➤➤ FEMME LISANT ◄◄

WHERE BOOKS FALL OPEN

A Reader's Anthology

of Wit & Passion

PAINTINGS BY

Bascove

DAVID R. GODINE · *Publisher*

BOSTON

In Memoriam
Lillian Hechter Bascove
and
Fred Marcellino

First published in 2001 by
David R. Godine, Publisher
Post Office Box 450
Jaffrey, New Hampshire 03452
www.godine.com

Anthology and illustrations copyright © 2001 by Bascove
Due to limitations of space, all permissions acknowledgments
appear on pages 145–150, which constitute
a continuation of the copyright page.

LIBRARY OF CONGRESS
CATALOGING-IN-PUBICATION DATA

Where books fall open : a reader's anthology
of wit and passion / painted and edited by Bascove
p.   cm.
ISBN 1–56792–186–6 (hardcover : alk. paper)
1. Books and reading—Fiction. I. Bascove

PN6120.95.B7 W49 2001
418´.4—dc21   2001040867

FIRST EDITION
Printed in Canada

CONTENTS

⌘

LOVERS OF READING

+>-+>-<-<-<-

THE WHITE PAGE

+>->->-<-<-<-<

SOME THIN LINE OF COMFORT

➤➤➤◄◄◄

WHERE BOOKS FALL OPEN

⇢⇥⇥⇤⇤⇠

LOVERS
OF
READING

–►–►–►–◄–◄–◄–

All good books have one thing in common — they are
truer than if they had really happened, and after
you have read one of them you will feel that
all that happened, happened to you and
then it belongs to you forever.

Ernest Hemingway

Literature is my Utopia. Here I am not disfranchised.
No barrier of the senses shuts me out from the sweet,
gracious discourse of my book-friends.

Helen Keller

Keep going; never stoop; sit tight;
Read something luminous at night.

Edmund Wilson

Sir, he hath not fed of the dainties that are bred of a book;
he hath not eat paper as it were; he hath not drunk ink:
his intellect is not replenished; he is only an animal,
only sensible in the duller parts.

William Shakespeare
LOVE'S LABOR'S LOST

–►–►–►–◄–◄–◄–

ITALO CALVINO

If On a Winter's Night a Traveler

In the shop window you have promptly identified the cover with the title you were looking for. Following this visual trail, you have forced your way through the shop past the thick barricade of Books You Haven't Read, which were frowning at you from the tables and shelves, trying to cow you. But you know you must never allow yourself to be awed, that among them there extend for acres and acres the Books You Needn't Read, the Books Made For Purposes Other Than Reading, Books Read Even Before You Open Them Since They Belong To The Category Of Books Read Before Being Written. And thus you pass the outer girdle of ramparts, but then you are attacked by the infantry of the Books That If You Had More Than One Life You Would Certainly Also Read But Unfortunately Your Days Are Numbered. With a rapid maneuver you bypass them and move into the phalanxes of the Books You Mean To Read But There Are Others You Must Read First, the Books Too Expensive Now And You'll Wait Till They're Remaindered, the Books ditto When They Come Out In Paperback, Books You Can Borrow From Somebody, Books That Everybody's Read So It's As If You Had Read Them, Too. Eluding these assaults, you come up beneath the towers of the fortress, where other troops are holding out:

the Books You've Been Planning To Read For Ages,

the Books You've Been Hunting For Years Without
Success,
the Books Dealing With Something You're Working
On At The Moment,
the Books You Want To Own So They'll Be Handy
Just In Case,
the Books You Could Put Aside Maybe To Read This
Summer,
the Books You Need To Go With Other Books On
Your Shelves,
the Books That Fill You With Sudden, Inexplicable
Curiosity, Not Easily Justified.

Now you have been able to reduce the countless embattled troops to an array that is, to be sure, very large but still calculable in a finite number; but this relative relief is then undermined by the ambush of the Books Read Long Ago Which It's Now Time To Reread and the Books You've Always Pretended To Have Read And Now It's Time To Sit Down And Really Read Them.

Ruined by Reading

We gaze at marks on a page, put there by a machine, recognizable as words. Each one denotes something discrete but we do not, cannot, read them as such, except in the first days of learning how. They offer themselves in groups with wholes greater than the sum of the parts. As in human groups, the individual members behave in relation to their companions: each word presents aspects of itself suited to the ambiance, amplifying some connotations and muting others. Their respective rankings must change too. A word will be key here, play a supporting role there, and in each successive appearance will be weightier and more richly nuanced. All this we register faster than the speed of the light illuminating our page, hardly aware of noting the valence, assessing the role and position, of each word as it flies by, granting it its place in the assemblage.

Still more remarkable, these inky marks generate emotion, even give the illusion of containing emotion, while it is we who contribute the emotion. Yet it was there in advance too, in the writer. What a feat of transmission: the emotive powers of the book, with no local habitation, pass safely from writer to reader, unmangled by printing and binding and shipping, renewed and available whenever we open it.

ROY BLOUNT, JR.

Summertime and the Reading Is Heavy

A feeling seems to have arisen that summer is the time for light reading. I don't know where anyone got that idea. The truth about summer is this. There are an enormous number of hours in it — slow hours — and yet, before you know it, somehow it is over. So all you have to do is to start reading Heidegger, say, on the first day of summer. One day you look up and both summer and Heidegger are done.

Summer is the time for heavy reading, reading that works up a sweat. I wouldn't be surprised if there were scientific studies showing that the sun's heat melts eye glaze. People are forever leaving Proust behind in summer cottages. "I was in the process of reading Proust from cover to cover to cover to cover last summer," people say all winter, "and then a lot of sand and coconut oil got in the part about Albertine and the dairy maid. . . . Tell me. This is something I've been wondering about. Is it your feeling that the dairy maid was actually a man, too?" But people do read *some* Proust in the summer. And next summer they find someone else's Proust in the new place they rent — a Proust in which nothing has been spilled — and they read some more.

Are people going to read Proust and make a living at the same time? No. Not ordinary people. Ordinary people are going to wait until they are at the beach, and the phone is not constantly ringing off the hook, and the only discouraging word is the sound of gulls squawking overhead.

That's when they are going to read Proust. Some Proust. Things feel heavier in the summer. Whatever you pursue in the summer is going to be heavy, even if it's Ed McBain. So it might as well be Melville's *Pierre, or The Ambiguities*. Which is not Proust, but does go on and on, and does have dialogue in it like this: "Can it? Can it? No — yes — surely — can it? It cannot be! . . . What can this bode?"

The thing to do is to set the summer aside, quite firmly, for all that heavy reading you have been meaning to get around to. "This summer I'm doing the deconstructionists." No one ever says, "This spring I'm doing the deconstructionists." Because in spring you are on the lookout for the first jonquil. I don't care what T. S. Eliot said about April, it is no time for the deconstructionists.

Summer is a different matter. The jonquils are finished. Your sunburn is such that the touch of a zephyr is like steel wool. In the summer you could read the *Cantos* of Ezra Pound. There is something unreal about the summer anyway, isn't there? Summer is when you see horseshoe crabs and Portuguese men-of-war. If these things exist in a civilized society, then why no great but completely insane poems about usury?

When it's summer, people sit a lot. Or lie. Lie in the sense of recumbency. A good heavy book holds you down. It's an anchor that keeps you from getting up and having another gin and tonic. Many a person has been saved from summer alcoholism, not to mention hypertoxicity, by Dostoyevsky. Put *The Idiot* in your lap or over your face, and you know where you are going to be for the afternoon.

What better time than summer for some really dense Faulkner? It's always hot in Mississippi, isn't it? Do you think you can make sense of *Light in August* in Connecticut in February? Do you think anything is light in August in Mississippi, or in Faulkner? Why do you think people write such hefty, seething stuff in South America? For two reasons: (1) Because they have read Faulkner. (2) Because it is hot in South America.

People evidently write in a kind of molten mode when it's hot. Profundity comes boiling up. It follows that people *read* in a kind of molten mode when it's hot. Profundity gets boiled right back down. No need to burn the midnight oil in summer. Heaviness can just be soaked up. I know a man who, in his youth, caddied for so many people who kept copies of *War and Peace* in their golf bags that when he was assigned that great novel in college (summer session, fortunately) he was able to read it in eleven days, which is four under par.

Russia is another interesting case. Russia is not known for being hot. And yet its literature is known for being heavy. Perhaps the truth is that heavy literature blooms in extremes of temperature. In most parts of this country, the closest we can come to the extremity of Russia's wintry cold is by lying out in the sun in July in the middle of the day at the beach. Pinned down helplessly by Goncharov's *Oblomov*.

But you say you have read all the heavy literature produced down through the ages. First, are you sure? You've read Sartre's *Being and Nothingness*? You've read it through a couple of times and sorted it all out, as to which is which? (Being is fall, winter, spring. Nothingness is summer.)

Okay. Here are the new heavy books for this summer's reading.

Imperfect Instincts, by Franz Glodz. The gravamen (a good summer word) of this demanding work is that the only way of living authentically is by getting in touch with

➤➤ QUIET CITY ◄◄

↠ LIBRARY ↞

one's instincts, bearing in mind that one's instincts are radically wrong, and exercising certain largely doomed corrective techniques. After reading this book, you may well not feel like doing anything. What better time to feel that way than in the summer? What is there to do in the summer anyway? Play tennis? Do you really think there is anything authentic, deep down, about your backhand?

Your Parents Didn't Love You, by Ciel LaVolf. Dr. LaVolf argues persuasively that your parents, at least if you were born before 1967, never really cared anything about you, and therefore they saddled you with a resentment toward them that you will carry to your grave and pass on to any children you may ill-advisedly have. Ignore Dr. LaVolf's message at your peril.

All About Flies, by Jo Tzwilitz. Sound like a lightweight subject? Not so. What Miss Tzwilitz has done here is get flies down, once and for all. In the process she answers such immemorial, swarmy-day questions as "What do flies want from me, anyway?" She has translated the language of flies, and given us access to "fly-arias" in which flies reveal, at droning length, that what they basically want to do is to eat something — just what, is not clear — in our hair.

This Was, by Garth Pflug. The subtitle of this 486-page confessional poem with no punctuation (except for one comma, which will make you jump and weep and forevermore appreciate commas) is *Even Harder on Me Than It's Going to Be on You but Not Much*. Enough said.

Life's Adjustable of Chaos, by Vliet Von Vargueles. You thought *Finnegan's Wake* drove you crazy? Did you keep thinking, while reading *Finnegan's Wake*, "If I could just come upon one straight phrase, even, that just sort of sounds like a normal person communicating"? Well, this new book is even more so, and longer. So rife is this new book with quintuple semi-entendres that if you could get cable television where you are, you would throw this book away. If the bluefish were biting where you are, you would throw this book away. If any halfway decent-looking sand dollars ever washed up where you are, you would throw this book away. And yet, you find yourself not throwing this book away. Because it is literally too heavy. And it costs $27.95. (Note: According to a rather pleading letter from the author's wife that was inserted in the review copy I received, the book's title is a pun on "Life is just a bowl of cherries.")

Holy Toledo, by Lembeck Thule. This is nothing less than an imagistic survey of the complete sprawling religious spectrum of Toledo, Ohio, presented as a kind of masque — now satirical, now theological, now dialectical, and always in dialect. Not exactly one's preconception of Ohioan speech sounds ("udge" is used for "of" throughout), but rather a whole new ecstatic language. Entire sermons, exactly as preached in actual Toledan services, are rendered as they would have sounded if anyone in Toledo actually spoke this way. It's tough going, but the effects are uncanny.

Uhhhhhh . . . Uhhh, by Hideyo Imi. A thirteenth-century Japanese epic poem, translated into English for the first time, which recounts the moving of Mount Ishi to the top of Mount Oh, boulder by boulder, by sumo wrestlers. The last 3,200 lines of this opus make the schlepping scenes in *The Naked and the Dead* seem downright airy, but a sprightly opening section gets you in the mood to put your shoulder to the task:

> *Welcome, distinguished reader. I would like you*
> *To read this mammoth epic instead of haiku.*

So slip on your goggles and your reading trunks, for the sun is high.

Let me leave you with one more thought. In what season of the year do we find ourselves — I'm speaking for a moment in terms of the physical world — *wading through* things?

Surf. Kelp. Books.

Summer.

Reading Something in the Restaurant

This morning I remembered the young man
with his book, reading at a table
by the window last night. Reading
amidst the coming and going of dishes
and voices. Now and then he looked
up and passed his finger across
his lips, as if pondering something,
or quieting the thoughts inside
his mind, the going
and coming inside his mind. Then
he lowered his head and went back
to reading. That memory
gets into my head this morning
with the memory of
the girl who entered the restaurant
that time long ago and stood shaking her hair.
Then sat down across from me
without taking her coat off.
I put down whatever book it was
I was reading, and she at once
started to tell me there was
not a snowball's chance in hell
this thing was going to fly.
She knew it. Then I came around
to knowing it. But it was

hard. This morning, my sweet,
you ask me what's new
in the world. But my concentration
is shot. At the table next
to ours a man laughs and laughs
and shakes his head at what
another fellow is telling him.
But what was that young man reading?
Where did that woman go?
I've lost my place. Tell me what it is
you wanted to know.

Listening to the Radio

We sit opposite each other in easy chairs, reading,
our feet touching on the hassock.
A story on Public Radio emerges from the wallpaper
of music. Our eyes lock, listening. Listening
we watch the story in the other's eyes, see each word
come at the same time.

Night swallows the walls of the room.
The story ends. We don't move.
Floor lamps next to our chairs
cast us in separate spheres of light. Is this
how we came into being? How one of us
will leave? Our eyes locked? How the one left will look

only death in the eye, the way the wolf and its prey
look at each other for a long moment
acknowledging the story, acknowledging the minute
the prey turns and runs the contract between them changes?
We return to our books, floating in the dark
like celestial bodies, a Bach partita supplying the ether.

KAREN CHAMBERS

❦

Reading Goals

When I was about five years old, I would walk by the glass-fronted mahogany bookcase in the living room. It was filled with books, a few porcelain figurines, a cut-glass bowl or two, and frequently a box of chocolates. That bookcase fascinated me and not just because I had a sweet-tooth and would steal a piece of candy when I passed. I longed to be able to read those books, to decipher what those strange symbols on the covers meant, to understand all of those words contained within. I suppose if I had been a brighter and more motivated child, I might have tried to learn to read on my own, or I might have convinced my mother to teach me, but I didn't. Instead I waited patiently to turn six and to start first grade.

As I learned to read, I would still pass that bookcase in wonder and made a vow that I would someday read all of those books. Most of them were popular novels, from the '30s and '40s, and as I grew up I was more interested in the Bobbsey Twins and Cherry Ames, a series of novels about a nurse, clearly intended to inspire young girls to pursue a medical career (in the '50s, girls aspired to be nurses and doctors' wives — MRS, not MDs). Later I read the classics that filled the reading lists of my English classes — Hawthorne, Melville, Dickens, the Brontës. On my own I read J. D. Salinger and Truman Capote. None of those books were in that bookcase.

When my mother moved to a retirement center, that bookcase was given to a cousin who had a Midwestern-sized house, a more congenial environment for it than a New York studio apartment. Since he didn't want them, I went through those books, all the ones I'd never read, and I discovered that there were none I really wanted to read as an adult. However, there was one that I kept, one that surprised me — after all it was my parents' bookcase — *The Kinsey Report*. Now it sits on my bookshelf, but it's still unread.

CHARLES SIMIC

The Pleasures of Reading

On his deathbed my father is reading
The memoirs of Casanova.
I'm watching the night fall,
A few windows being lit across the street.
In one of them a young woman is reading
Close to the glass.
She hasn't looked up in a long while,
Even with the darkness coming.

While there's still a bit of light,
I want her to lift her head,
So I can see her face
Which I have already imagined,
But her book must be full of suspense.
And besides, it's so quiet,
Every time she turns a page,
I can hear my father turn one too,
As if they are reading the same book.

The Library in the Garret

Books, books, books!
I had found the secret of a garret-room
Piled high with cases in my father's name;
Piled high, packed large, — where, creeping in and out
Among the giant fossils of my past,
Like some small nimble mouse between the ribs
Of a mastodon, I nibbled here and there
At this or that box, pulling through the gap,
In heats of terror, haste, victorious joy,
The first book first. And how I felt it beat
Under my pillow, in the morning's dark,
An hour before the sun would let me read!
My books!

✦

The Back Bedroom

"Flushie," wrote Miss Barrett, "is my friend — my companion — and loves me better than he loves the sunshine without." She could not go out. She was chained to the sofa. "A bird in a cage would have as good a story," she wrote, as she had. And Flush, to whom the whole world was free, chose to forfeit all the smells of Wimpole Street in order to lie by her side.

And yet sometimes the tie would almost break; there were vast gaps in their understanding. Sometimes they would lie and stare at each other in blank bewilderment. Why, Miss Barrett wondered, did Flush tremble suddenly, and whimper and start and listen? She could hear nothing; she could see nothing; there was nobody in the room with them. She could not guess that Folly, her sister's little King Charles, had passed the door; or that Catiline, the Cuba bloodhound, had been given a mutton-bone by a footman in the basement. But Flush knew; he heard; he was ravaged by the alternate rages of lust and greed....

Flush was equally at a loss to account for Miss Barrett's emotions. There she would lie hour after hour passing her hand over a white page with a black stick; and her eyes would suddenly fill with tears; but why?... But there was no sound in the room, no smell to make Miss Barrett cry. Then again Miss Barrett, still agitating her stick, burst out laughing.... What was there to laugh at in the black smudge that she held out for Flush to look at? He could smell nothing; he could hear nothing. There was nobody in the room with them. The fact was that they could not communicate with words, and it was a fact that led undoubtedly to much misunderstanding. Yet did it not lead also to a peculiar intimacy? "Writing," — Miss Barrett once exclaimed after a morning's toil, "writing, writing. . ." After all, she may have thought, do words say everything? Can words say anything? Do not words destroy the symbol that lies beyond the reach of words?. . .

When he heard her low voice syllabling innumerable sounds, he longed for the day when his own rough roar would issue like hers in the little simple sounds that had such mysterious meaning. And when he watched the same fingers for ever crossing a white page with a straight stick, he longed for the time when he too should blacken paper as she did.

And yet, had he been able to write as she did? — The question is superfluous happily, for truth compels us to say that in the year 1842–43 Miss Barrett was not a nymph but an invalid; Flush was not a poet but a red cocker spaniel; and Wimpole Street was not Arcady but Wimpole Street.

UMBERTO ECO

⚜

How to Organize a Public Library

1. The various catalogues must be housed as far apart as possible from one another. All care must be taken to separate the catalogue of books from that of periodicals, and these two from the catalogue by subject; similarly, the recent acquisitions must be kept well away from older collections. If possible, the spelling in the two catalogues (recent acquisitions and older collections) must be different. In recent acquisitions, for example, *pajama* should be spelled with an *a*, in the older, *pyjama* with a *y*. *Chaĭkovskiĭ* in recent acquisitions will follow the Library of Congress system; in the older catalogue the name will be spelled in the old-fashioned way, with *Tch*.

2. The subjects must be determined by the librarian. On their copyright pages the books must bear no indication of the subjects under which they are to be listed.

3. Call numbers should be impossible to decipher and, if possible, very complex, so that anyone filling out a call slip will never have room to include the last line of numbers and will assume they are irrelevant. Then the desk attendant will hand the slip back to him with the admonition to fill it out properly.

4. The time between request and delivery must be as long as possible.

5. Only one book should be released at a time.

6. The books distributed by the attendant after the request

form has been properly submitted cannot be taken into the reference room, so the scholars must divide their working life into two fundamental aspects: reading on the one hand, and reference consultation on the other. The library must discourage, as conducive to strabismus, any crossover tendencies or attempts at the simultaneous reading of several books.

7. Insofar as possible, no photocopier should be available; if such a machine does exist, access to it must be made very time-consuming and toilsome, fees should be higher than those in any neighborhood copy shop, and the maximum number of copied pages permitted should not exceed two or three.

8. The librarian must consider the reader an enemy, a waster of time (otherwise he or she would be at work), and a potential thief.

9. The reference librarian's office must be impregnable.

10. Loans must be discouraged.

11. Interlibrary loans must be impossible or, at best, must require months. The ideal course, in any event, is to ensure the impossibility of discovering the contents of other libraries.

12. Given this policy, theft must be very easy.

13. Opening hours must coincide precisely with local office hours, determined by foresighted discussions with trade union officials and the Chamber of Commerce; total closing on Saturday, Sunday, evenings and mealtimes goes without saying. The library's worst enemy is the employed student; its best friend is Thomas Jefferson, someone who has a large personal library and therefore no need to visit the public library (to which he may nevertheless bequeath his books at his death).

14. It must be impossible to find any refreshment inside the library, under any circumstances; and it must also be impossible to leave the library to seek sustenance elsewhere without first returning all books in use, so that, after having a cup of coffee, the student must fill out requests for them again.
15. It must be impossible on a given day to find the book one had been using the day before.
16. It must be impossible to learn who has a book that it currently out on loan.
17. If possible, no rest rooms.
18. Ideally, the reader should be unable to enter the library. If he does actually enter, exploiting with tedious insistence a right, granted on the basis of the principles of 1789, that has nevertheless not been assimilated by the collective sensibility, he must never ever — with the exception of rapid visits to the reference shelves — be allowed access to the sanctum of the stacks.

CONFIDENTIAL NOTE: All staff must be affected by physical defects, as it is the duty of a public institution to offer job opportunities to handicapped citizens (the Fire Department is considering an extension of this rule to their ranks). In particular, the ideal librarian should limp, in order to lengthen the time devoted to receiving the call slip, descending into the basement, and returning. For personnel expected to use ladders to reach the shelves more than eight meters above the ground, it is required that missing arms be replaced by prosthetic hooks, for security reasons. Personnel lacking both upper limbs will deliver the requested volume by gripping it in their teeth (library regulations tend to prevent the delivery of volumes in a format larger than octavo).

Ethereal Mildness

March 24, 1928

Oh, I feel terrible. Rotten, I feel. I've got Spring Misery. I've got a mean attack of Crocus Urge. I bet you I'm running a temperature right at this moment; running it ragged. I ought to be in bed, that's where I ought to be. Not that it would do any good if I were. I can't sleep. I can't sleep for a damn. I can't sleep for sour apples. I can't sleep for you and who else.

I'm always this way in the Spring. Sunk in Springtime: or Take Away Those Violets. I hate the filthy season. Summer makes me drowsy, Autumn makes me sing, Winter's pretty lousy, but I hate Spring. They know how I feel. They know what Spring makes out of me. Just a Thing That Was Once a Woman, that's all I am in the Springtime. But do they do anything about it? Oh, no. Not they. Every year, back Spring comes, with the nasty little birds yapping their fool heads off, and the ground all mucked up with arbutus. Year after year after year. And me not able to sleep, on account of misery. All right, Spring. Go ahead and laugh your girlish laughter, you big sap. Funny, isn't it? People with melancholic insomnia are screams, aren't they? You just go on and laugh yourself simple. That's the girl!

It isn't as if I hadn't tried practically every way I ever heard of to induce sleep. I've taken long walks around the room in the midnight silence, and I've thought soothing thoughts, and I've recited long passages of poetry; I have even tried counting Van Dorens. But nothing works, drugs nor anything else. Not poppy nor mandragora. There was a book called *Not Poppy*, and now there's one called *Not Magnolia*, and is it any wonder a person goes crazy? What with Spring and book titles and loss of sleep, acute melancholia is the least I could have. I'm having a bad time. Oh, awful.

There has been but one sweet, misty interlude in my long stretch of white nights. That was the evening I fell into a dead dreamless slumber brought on by the reading of a book called *Appendicitis*. (Well, picture my surprise when this turned out to be a book review, after all! You could have knocked me over with a girder.) *Appendicitis* is the work of Thew Wright, A.B., M.D., F.A.C.S., who has embellished his pages with fascinatingly anatomical illustrations, and has remarked, in his dedication, that he endeavors through this book to bring an understanding of appendicitis to the laity. And it is really terribly hard to keep from remarking, "That was no laity; that's my wife." It is hard, but I'll do it if it kills me.

You might, and with good reasons, take for your favorite picture the "Front View of the Abdominal Cavity." It is good, I admit; it has nice nuances, there is rhythm to the composition, and clever management is apparent in the shadows. But my feeling is that it is a bit sentimental, a little pretty-pretty, too obviously done with an eye toward popularity. It may well turn out to be another "Whistler's Mother" or a "Girl with Fan." My own choice is the impression of "Vertical Section of Peritoneum." It has strength, simplicity, delicacy, pity, and irony. Perhaps, I grant you, my judgment is influenced by my sentiment for the subject. For who that has stood, bareheaded, and beheld the Peritoneum by moonlight can gaze unmoved upon its likeness?

The view of the Peritoneum induces waking dreams, but not slumber. For that I had to get into the text of the book. In his preface, Dr. Wright observes that "The chapter on anatomy, while it may appear formidable, will, it is believed, well repay the reader for his effort in reading it." Ever anxious to be well repaid, I turned to the chapter. It did appear formidable; it appeared as formidable as all get-out. And when I saw that it started "Let us divide the abdominal cavity into four parts by means of four imaginary lines," I could only murmur, "Ah, let's don't. Surely we can think up something better to play than that."

From there, I went skipping about through the book, growing ever more blissfully weary. Only once did I sit up sharply, and dash sleep from my lids. That was at the section having to do with the love-life of poisonous bacteria. That, says the author, "is very simple and consists merely of the bacterium dividing into two equal parts." Think of it — no quarrels, no lies, no importunate telegrams, no unanswered letters. Just peace and sunshine and quiet evenings around the lamp. Probably bacteria sleep like logs. Why shouldn't they? What is Spring to them?

And, at the end of twenty-four hours, the happy couple — or the happy halves, if you'd rather — will have 16,772,216 children to comfort them in their old age. Who would not be proud to have 16,772,216 little heads clustered about his knee, who would not be soothed and safe to think of the young people carrying on the business after the old folks have passed on? I wish, I wish I were a poisonous bacterium. Yes, and I know right now where I'd go to bring up my family, too. I've got that all picked out. What a time I'd show *him!*

Barring the passages dealing with the life and times of bacteria, there is nothing in Dr. Wright's work to block repose. It is true that I never did find out whether I really had appendicitis — which is why I ever started the book, anyway — or whether it was just the effects of that new Scotch of mine which, friends tell me, must have been specially made by the Borgias. But *Appendicitis* gave me a few blessed hours of forgetfulness, and for that I am almost cringingly grateful to Thew Wright, A.B., M.D., F.A.C.S., and all-around good fellow.

ROBERTSON DAVIES

Books Are for Reading

As I said at the beginning, if you have ten books which you have acquired because you truly want them, you are a collector and your library is in some degree a portrait of you. But few people with the book mania reckon their books in tens; they count them in hundreds and thousands. If you read a great deal you will almost certainly want some books which are out of the ordinary, because of their rarity or beauty. It is at this point that I beg you to be careful. You will be tempted to think of books as objects, not to be read, but to be possessed for show, and when that happens, you are easy prey to those booksellers who deal in harlot volumes, tricked out in pretty skins (which will not last because the leather is not well prepared) and bedizened with gold ornament which resembles nothing so much as the gold paint that used to be daubed on steam-heating coils. All the arts of the horse dealer will be exercised to make old books which are of slight value look like treasures. And if you fall for this trash, you will at last have an accumulation which looks like the background for one of those advertisement pictures in which a model is impersonating an advertising man's notion of a gentleman and a scholar drinking Somebody's whisky. It will not be a library at all, but an adjunct of that pompous buffoonery which is called, by its dupes, "gracious living." You will be surrounded by a bad stage setting, and its effect will be to turn you into a bad actor.

You will have committed the great sin of our time, which is to put ends before means, and striving and competition will become more important to you than reading. Be ambitious, rather, to be able to say as a reader what Hilaire Belloc said as a writer:

When I am dead, I hope it may be said:
"His sins were scarlet, but his books were read."

Never Do That to a Book

When I was eleven and my brother was thirteen, our parents took us to Europe. At the Hôtel d'Angleterre in Copenhagen, as he had done virtually every night of his literate life, Kim left a book facedown on the bedside table. The next afternoon, he returned to find the book closed, a piece of paper inserted to mark the page, and the following note, signed by the chambermaid, resting on its cover:

SIR, YOU MUST NEVER DO THAT TO A BOOK.

My brother was stunned. How could it have come to pass that he — a reader so devoted that he'd sneaked a book and a flashlight under the covers at his boarding school every night after lights-out, a crime punishable by a swat with a wooden paddle — had been branded as *someone who didn't love books?* I shared his mortification. I could not imagine a more bibliolatrous family than the Fadimans. Yet, with the exception of my mother, in the eyes of the young Danish maid we would all have been found guilty of rampant book abuse.

During the next thirty years I came to realize that just as there is more than one way to love a person, so is there more than one way to love a book. The chambermaid believed in courtly love. A book's physical self was sacrosanct to her, its form inseparable from its content; her duty as a lover was Platonic adoration, a noble but doomed attempt to conserve forever the state of perfect chastity in which it had left the bookseller. The Fadiman family believed in carnal love. To us, a book's *words* were holy, but the paper, cloth, cardboard, glue, thread, and ink that contained them were a mere vessel, and it was no sacrilege to treat them as wantonly as desire and pragmatism dictated. Hard use was a sign not of disrespect but of intimacy.

Hilaire Belloc, a courtly lover, once wrote:

> *Child! do not throw this book about;*
> *Refrain from the unholy pleasure*
> *Of cutting all the pictures out!*
> *Preserve it as your chiefest treasure.*

What would Belloc have thought of my father, who, in order to reduce the weight of the paperbacks he read on airplanes, tore off the chapters he had completed and threw them in the trash? What would he have thought of my husband, who reads in the sauna, where heat-fissioned pages drop like petals in a storm? What would he have thought (here I am making a brazen attempt to upgrade my family by association) of Thomas Jefferson, who chopped up a priceless 1572 first edition of Plutarch's works in Greek in order to interleave its pages with an English translation? Or of my old editor Byron Dobell, who, when he was researching an article on the Grand Tour, once stayed up all night reading six volumes of Boswell's journals and, as he puts it, "sucked them like a giant mongoose"? Byron told me, "I didn't give a damn about the condition of those volumes. In order to get where I had to go, I underlined them, wrote in them, shredded them, dropped them, tore them to pieces, and did things to them that we can't discuss in public."

Byron loves books. Really, he does. So does my husband, an incorrigible book-splayer whose roommate once informed him, "George, if you ever break the spine of one of my books, I want you to know you might as well be breaking *my own spine.*" So does Kim, who reports that despite his experience in Copenhagen, his bedside table currently supports three spreadeagled volumes. "They are ready in an instant to let me pick them up," he explains. "To use an electronics analogy, closing a book on a bookmark is like pressing the Stop button, whereas when you leave the book facedown, you've only pressed Pause." I confess to marking my place promiscuously, sometimes splaying, sometimes committing the even more grievous sin of dog-earing the page. (Here I manage to be simultaneously abusive and compulsive: I turn down the upper corner for page-marking and the lower corner to identify passages I want to xerox for my commonplace book.)

All courtly lovers press Stop. My Aunt Carol — who will probably claim she's no relation once she finds out how I treat my books — places reproductions of Audubon paintings horizontally to mark the exact paragraph where she left off. If the colored side is up, she was reading the lefthand page; if it's down, the right-hand page. A college classmate of mine, a lawyer, uses his business cards, spurning his wife's silver Tiffany bookmarks because they are a few microns too thick and might leave vestigial stigmata. Another classmate, an art historian, favors Paris Métro tickets or "those inkjet-printed credit card receipts — but only in books of art criticism whose pretentiousness I wish to desecrate with something really crass and financial. I would never use those in fiction or poetry, which really *are* sacred."

Courtly lovers always remove their bookmarks when the

assignation is over; carnal lovers are likely to leave romantic mementos, often three-dimensional and messy. *Birds of Yosemite and the East Slope*, a volume belonging to a science writer friend, harbors an owl feather and the tip of a squirrel's tail, evidence of a crime scene near Tioga Pass. A book critic I know took *The Collected Stories and Poems* of Edgar Allan Poe on a backpacking trip through the Yucatan, and whenever an interesting bug landed in it, she clapped the covers shut. She amassed such a bulging insectarium that she feared Poe might not make it through customs. (He did.)

The most permanent, and thus to the courtly lover the most terrible, thing one can leave in a book is one's own words. Even I would never write in an encyclopedia (except perhaps with a No. 3 pencil, which I'd later erase). But I've been annotating novels and poems — transforming monologues into dialogues — ever since I learned to read. Byron Dobell says that his most beloved books, such as *The Essays of Montaigne*, have been written on so many times, in so many different periods of his life, in so many colors of ink, that they have become palimpsests. I would far rather read Byron's copy of Montaigne than a virginal one from the bookstore, just as I would rather read John Adams's copy of Mary Wollstonecraft's *French Revolution*, in whose margins he argued so vehemently with the dead author ("Heavenly times!" "A barbarous theory." "Did this lady think three months time enough to form a free constitution for twenty-five millions of Frenchmen?") that, two hundred years later, his handwriting still looks angry.

Just think what courtly lovers miss by believing that the only thing they are permitted to do with books is *read* them! What do they use for shims, doorstops, gluing weights, and rug-flatteners? When my friend the art historian was a teenager, his cherished copy of *D'Aulaire's Book of Greek Myths* served as a drum pad on which he practiced percussion riffs from Led Zeppelin. A philosophy professor at my college, whose baby became enamored of the portrait of David Hume on a Penguin paperback, had the cover laminated in plastic so her daughter could cut her teeth on the great thinker. Menelik II, the emperor of Ethiopia at the turn of the century, liked to chew pages from his Bible. Unfortunately, he died after consuming the complete Book of Kings. I do not consider Menelik's fate an argument for keeping our hands and teeth off our books; the lesson to be drawn, clearly, is that he, too, should have laminated his pages in plastic.

THE WHITE PAGE

‑‑≻‑‑≻‑≺‑‑≺‑‑≺‑

Writing and reading are not all that distinct for a writer.
Both exercises require being alert and ready for
unaccountable beauty, for the intricateness or
simple elegance of the writer's imagination,
for the world that imagination evokes.

Toni Morrison

No sooner is the ink dry than it revolts me.

Beckett

Only describe what you have seen. Look long and hard
at the things that please you, even longer and harder
at what causes you pain.

Colette

There are three rules for writing the novel.
Unfortunately, no one knows what they are.

W. Somerset Maugham

‑‑≻‑‑≻‑≺‑‑≺‑‑≺‑

MURIEL RUKEYSER

Poem   White   Page
White   Page   Poem

Poem   white page   white page   poem
something is streaming out of a body in waves
something is beginning from the fingertips
they are starting to declare for my whole life
all the despair and the making music
something like wave after wave
that breaks on a beach
something like bringing the entire life
to this moment
the small waves bringing themselves to white paper
something like light stands up and is alive

Purity

My favorite time to write is in the late afternoon,
weekdays, particularly Wednesdays.
This is how I go about it:
I take a fresh pot of tea into my study and close the door.
Then I remove my clothes and leave them in a pile
as if I had melted to death and my legacy consisted of only
a white shirt, a pair of pants and a pot of cold tea.

Then I remove my flesh and hang it over a chair.
I slide it off my bones like a silken garment.
I do this so that what I write will be pure,
completely rinsed of the carnal,
uncontaminated by the preoccupations of the body.

Finally I remove each of my organs and arrange them
on a small table near the window.
I do not want to hear their ancient rhythms
when I am trying to tap out my own drumbeat.

Now I sit down at the desk, ready to begin.
I am entirely pure: nothing but a skeleton at a typewriter.

I should mention that sometimes I leave my penis on.
I find it difficult to ignore the temptation.
Then I am a skeleton with a penis at a typewriter.

In this condition I write extraordinary love poems,
most of them exploiting the connection between sex and
        death.

I am concentration itself: I exist in a universe
where there is nothing but sex, death, and typewriting.

After a spell of this I remove my penis too.
Then I am all skull and bones typing into the afternoon.
Just the absolute essentials, no flounces.
Now I write only about death, most classical of themes
in language light as the air between my ribs.

Afterward, I reward myself by going for a drive at sunset.
I replace my organs and slip back into my flesh
and clothes. Then I back the car out of the garage
and speed through woods on winding country roads,
passing stone walls, farmhouses, and frozen ponds,
all perfectly arranged like words in a famous sonnet.

The Joy of Writing

Why does this written doe bound through these written
    woods?
For a drink of written water from a spring
whose surface will xerox her soft muzzle?
Why does she lift her head; does she hear something?
Perched on four slim legs borrowed from the truth,
she pricks up her ears beneath my fingertips.
Silence — this word also rustles across the page
and parts the boughs
that have sprouted from the word "woods."

Lying in wait, set to pounce on the blank page,
are letters up to no good,
clutches of clauses so subordinate
they'll never let her get away.

Each drop of ink contains a fair supply
of hunters, equipped with squinting eyes behind their
    sights,
prepared to swarm the sloping pen at any moment,
surround the doe, and slowly aim their guns.

They forget that what's here isn't life.
Other laws, black on white, obtain.
The twinkling of an eye will take as long as I say,
and will, if I wish, divide into tiny eternities,
full of bullets stopped in mid-flight.

✦➤ CAT WITH NUDES ◄✦

➤➤ WOMEN AND FICTION ➤➤

Not a thing will ever happen unless I say so.
Without my blessing, not a leaf will fall,
not a blade of grass will bend beneath that little hoof's full
      stop.

Is there then a world
where I rule absolutely on fate?
A time I bind with chains of signs?
An existence become endless at my bidding?

The joy of writing.
The power of preserving.
Revenge of a mortal hand.

ANNA AKHMATOVA

The Poet

Some job, you'll think — not such a dumb thing,
A life with a trouble-free run:
Hear music, pick up from it something
And call it your own in fun.

And somebody's light-hearted scherzo
Do up into stanzas and feet,
And swear that the poor heart hurts so
And moans 'mid the glittering wheat.

Then walk in the wood, overhearing
The firs that look slow of speech,
While smokescreen-like in the clearing
The fog covers all within reach.

Right, left, here a jot, there a tittle,
I dare even draw, as of right,
From devious life just a little,
And all — from the hush of the night.

Afternoon in the House

It's quiet here. The cats
sprawl, each
in a favored place.
The geranium leans this way
to see if I'm writing about her:
head all petals, brown
stalks, and those green fans.
So you see,
I am writing about you.

I turn on the radio. Wrong.
Let's not have any noise
in this room, except
the sound of a voice reading a poem.
The cat's request
The Meadow Mouse, by Theodore Roethke.

The house settles down on its haunches
for a doze.
I know you are with me, plants,
and cats — and even so, I'm frightened,
sitting in the middle of perfect
possibility.

RAINER MARIA RILKE

The Notebooks of Maulte Laurids Brigge

Ah! but verses amount to so little when one writes them young. One ought to wait and gather sense and sweetness a whole life long, and a long life if possible, and then, quite at the end, one might perhaps be able to write ten lines that were good. For verses are not, as people imagine, simply feelings (those one has early enough), — they are experiences. For the sake of a single verse, one must see many cities, men and things, one must know the animals, one must feel how the birds fly and know the gesture with which the little flowers open in the morning. One must be able to think back to roads in unknown regions, to unexpected meetings and to partings one had long seen coming; to days of childhood that are still unexplained, to parents whom one had to hurt when they brought one some joy and one did not grasp it (it was a joy for someone else); to childhood illnesses that so strangely begin with such a number of profound and grave transformations, to days in rooms withdrawn and quiet and to mornings by the sea, to the sea itself, to seas, to nights of travel that rushed along on high and flew with all the stars — and it is not yet enough if one may think of all this. One must have memories of many nights of love, none of which was like the others, of the screams of women in labor, and of light, white, sleeping women in childbed, closing again. But one must also have been beside the dying, must have sat beside the dead in the room with the open window and the fitful noises. And still it is not yet enough to have memories. One must be able to forget them when they are many and one must have the great patience to wait until they come again. For it is not yet the memories themselves. Not till they have turned to blood within us, to glance and gesture, nameless and no longer to be distinguished from ourselves — not till then can it happen that in a most rare hour the first word of a verse arises in their midst and goes forth from them.

QIN ZIHAO

❧

Seeds of Poetry

Will locks itself in a tiny room
An immense world in the room

A song of the century drifts by the ears
A roaring flame burns in the chest

It projects ideals onto blank paper
Sowing seeds of fire in the squares

Seeds of fire are a skyful of stars
All falling on the dark earth

When seeds of fire light up human hearts
It bids a smiling farewell to the world

LANGSTON HUGHES

Theme for English B

The instructor said,

> *Go home and write*
> *a page tonight.*
> *And let that page come out of you —*
> *Then, it will be true.*

I wonder if it's that simple?
I am twenty-two, colored, born in Winston-Salem.
I went to school there, then Durham, then here
to this college on the hill above Harlem.
I am the only colored student in my class.
The steps from the hill lead down into Harlem,
through a park, then I cross St. Nicholas,
Eighth Avenue, Seventh, and I come to the Y,
the Harlem Branch Y, where I take the elevator
up to my room, sit down, and write this page:

It's not easy to know what is true for you or me
at twenty-two, my age. But I guess I'm what
I feel and see and hear, Harlem, I hear you:
hear you, hear me — we two — you, me, talk on this page.
(I hear New York, too.) Me — who?
Well, I like to eat, sleep, drink, and be in love.
I like to work, read, learn, and understand life.
I like a pipe for a Christmas present,
or records — Bessie, bop, or Bach.

I guess being colored doesn't make me *not* like
the same things other folks like who are other races.
So will my page be colored that I write?
Being me, it will not be white.
But it will be
a part of you, instructor.
You are white —
yet a part of me, as I am a part of you.
That's American.
Sometimes perhaps you don't want to be a part of me.
Nor do I often want to be a part of you.
But we are, that's true!
As I learn from you,
I guess you learn from me —
although you're older — and white —
and somewhat more free.

This is my page for English B.

CALVIN TRILLIN

Opportunities in Poetry

Most poems aren't in magazines at all.
You see them scrawled in pencil on a stall.
A poet must feel grateful writing for
Most any place where MEN's not on the door —
Especially any place that pays a fee
That varies just a tiny bit from free.

Word

I'm going to crumple this word,
to twist it,
yes,
it's too slick
like a big dog or a river
had been lapping it down with its tongue, or water
had worn it away with the years.

I want gravel
to show in the word,
the ferruginous salt,
the gap-toothed power
of the soil.
There must be a blood-letting
for talker and non-talker alike.

I want to see thirst
in the syllables,
touch fire
in the sound;
feel through the dark
for the scream. Let
my words be acrid
as virginal stone.

JEROME CHARYN

Word Music

I think of the word *music*, because that seems much more basic than sentences or even a narrative song. The lilt, the feel, the sound of word upon word. And those terrifying white spaces between the words. That is the only aesthetic I know. Sound and silence, silence and sound. And those tales that have magicked me with their marvelous openings, like Faulkner's Benjy looking through the "curling flower spaces," or Humbert Humbert fiddling with Lolita's name like some madman inside a tent.

The narrative coheres and curls against the ribs of sound. Images form. We bump from page to page. Suddenly we have a story. I'm not sure why. *Lolita* is nothing more than Nabokov's music. I think of Isaak Babel. Why do his stories "sing" to us, even through the muddle of translation? Perhaps Babel's music is so near the surface — both skeleton and skin — that it survives a translator's reductive voice. And we fall in love with Benya Krik, that Odessa gangster in orange pants, who is as melodious as any male soprano. I can read Babel again and again, because that childlike wonder *and* music are always in the text.

I defy anyone to discover *one* unmusical sentence in all of James Joyce. Even that awful prig, Dedalus, has his own collapsible song. The meaning of a text is its music. What is *Tristram Shandy* all about, but the babble of an unborn child? And when the music fails, a text begins to die. That's why Dickens is such a marvelous, schizoid writer. He either tickles you to death, or lulls you into a morbid, terrifying sleep.

As for myself, I will look at a certain novel, say *Going to Jerusalem*, and the music isn't there. I look at another, and I can feel a merciless, driving wit. They're all failures, those novels of mine, but so what? I still have some music in my head. I sharpen my pencils, begin a new book, fall into a rocking mountain of words. . . .

~❦~

This Monkey, My Back

For a long while there, I was a young writer, and then, for nearly as long, I was a *younger* writer (younger than whom, I used to wonder — Robert Frost?). Now I'm just a writer. Certainly not an old writer, no *éminence gris*, no member of the Academy with yellowed hairs growing out of my ears and nostrils, but a writer, I like to think, of wisdom and maturity, with a few good years left ahead of me. Still, I had a shock a couple of months ago, when an old friend stopped by on his way back from Mexico and revealed something to me about the age we'd attained — or were rapidly approaching. We were sitting at the kitchen table, and he'd just fanned out a group of photographs and narrated the story of each one: I saw the Zócalo, the soap-powder beaches of Puerto Escondido, the catacombs beneath some ancient church. There was a pause, and then he said, "You know, in a couple of years I'm thinking of retiring." I was stunned. This was a vigorous man of forty-nine, a snappy dresser who'd made good money in his own business. "Retire?" I gasped, summoning up ghosts in carpet slippers hunkered before the TV at eleven A.M. and slurping up lime Jell-O and bourbon. All I could think to do was fish through the glossy photos before me till I found the one of the catacombs, shrunken tanned hides and lipless teeth, the claws that used to be fingers, people laid out on slabs like fallen trees. I held it up. "This is my retirement," I told him.

James Baldwin said that we write to give order and structure to a chaotic world, and this is surely part of it, maybe
the biggest part, but there's more to it than that. Writing is
a habit, an addiction, as powerful and overmastering an
urge as putting a bottle to your lips or a spike in your arm.
Call it the impulse to make something out of nothing, call it
an obsessive-compulsive disorder, call it logorrhea. Have
you been in a bookstore lately? Have you seen what these
authors are doing, the mountainous piles of the flakes of
themselves they're leaving behind, like the neatly labeled
jars of shit, piss, and toenail clippings one of Vonnegut's
characters bequeathed to his wife, the ultimate expression
of his deepest self? Retire? Retire from *that?* Sure, we'll all
retire, all of us, once they drain our blood and pump the
embalming fluid in.

EDNA ST. VINCENT MILLAY

If I Die Solvent

If I die solvent — die, that is to say,
In full possession of my critical mind,
Not having cast, to keep the wolves at bay
In this dark wood — till all be flung behind —
Wit, courage, honour, pride, oblivion
Of the red eyeball and the yellow tooth;
Nor sweat nor howl nor break into a run
When loping Death's upon me in hot sooth;
'Twill be that in my honoured hands I bear
What's under no condition to be spilled
Till my blood spills and hardens in the air:
An earthen grail, a humble vessel filled
To its low brim with water from that brink
Where Shakespeare, Keats and Chaucer learned to drink.

Poetry's Value

If you ask me abruptly
Why write poetry
Why not do
Something useful
Then I won't know
How to answer you
I am like a goldsmith hammering day and night
Just so I can extend pain
Into a gold ornament as thin as a cicada's wing
I don't know if working so hard
To transform sorrows into
Shimmering words and phrases
Is also
Beautifully worthwhile.

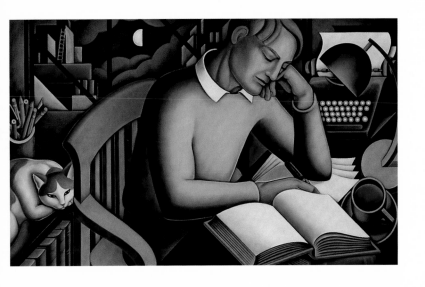

LA LUNE EN HIVER

→→ MOTHER AND CHILD READING ←←

MARY GORDON

My Curtains: Snowbound

I am working in my bedroom, which I have never before done. Writing a poem, which I rarely do. Both the place where I write and what I am writing are a way of getting back slowly.

As I work in this room, it takes on for me the feeling of sanctuary. I like to sit down at the window and look at my pretty curtains, light blue and white — the blue a faded dream color, the flowers fleurs-de-lis or mulberries, the border blue-gray chrysanthemums. The street shines with rain. I look out at the house across the street — a red ranch, low, emblematic of 1950s happiness. I like the family that lives there. The father and I talk about dogs.

Now it has gone nearly dark; it is nearly seven o'clock. In ten minutes I will have to go downstairs. Back to the life of the family, which flares below, flame-colored. While here, in this room — made secret by these curtains, by the very fact that it is where I am working — the light is matte. I haven't enough time left to do what I wanted to do today, but it's my own fault; instead of writing when I could have looked out as the rain became snow, grew heavy, then blue from its own weight, I spoke on the phone. I should not have answered the phone. And now that light is lost forever. I will not be able to describe it as I might have had I looked at it and written as I looked. I ought to be longing for spring, but it is winter light I find the most congenial.

It has snowed so much this hour that I know we are snowbound for this night. It is a feeling I like, the snow at once isolating and enclosing. I like it because this is the weather most like motherhood.

from *Having a Baby, Finishing a Book*

The Poet

She is working now, in a room
not unlike this one,
the one where I write, or you read.
Her table is covered with paper.
The light of the lamp would be
tempered by a shade, where the bulb's
single harshness might dissolve,
but it is not, she has taken it off.
Her poems? I will never know them,
though they are the ones I most need.
Even the alphabet she writes in
I cannot decipher. Her chair —
Let us imagine whether it is leather
or canvas, vinyl or wicker. Let her
have a chair, her shadeless lamp,
the table. Let one or two she loves
be in the next room. Let the door
be closed, the sleeping ones healthy.
Let her have time, and silence,
enough paper to make mistakes and go on.

❧

An Old Prayer

*A person to be writing a tale, and to find that it shapes
itself against his intentions; that the characters act otherwise than he thought; that unforeseen events occur; and a
catastrophe comes which he strives in vain to avert. It
might shadow forth his own fate, — he having made
himself one of the personages.*

— Hawthorne, *American Notebooks*, 1835

The stories that require telling. The stories that insist
upon their telling. Bud and flower in the brain and crack
the brain like concrete. The syllables, the words,
the intoxication of ink, the old mossy tales,
engraved in stone.

Crossing the room just now you experiment inviting
a story: the high-polished floor, the rap of the heels,
a stir of seductive curtains at the window, the moon
curved small as a fingernail.
If you lean out the window to seize the moon:
a story, an ancient story, teeth sinking
in your throat.
Don't imagine you are master.
You are never master.

And how must it end? you ask.

MARGARET ATWOOD

Psalm to Snake

O snake, you are an argument
for poetry:

a shift among dry leaves
when there is no wind,
a thin line moving through

that which is not
time, creating time,
a voice from the dead, oblique

and silent. A movement
from left to right,
a vanishing. Prophet under a stone.

I know you're there
even when I can't see you

I see the trail you make
in the blank sand, in the morning

I see the point
of intersection, the whiplash
across the eye. I see the kill.

O long word, cold-blooded and perfect

STEVE MARTIN

~ↄᴋ~

A Word from the Words

First, let me say how much I enjoy being one of the words in this book and how grateful I am for this opportunity to speak for the whole group. Often we're so busy speaking for others that we never get to speak for ourselves, or directly to you, the reader. I guess it's redundant to say "you, the reader," but we're not used to writing, and it sounds better to my ear than, say, "you, the two giant fists that are holding me" or "you, the large, heavy mass of protoplasm."

There's also a nice variety of words in this book, and that always makes it fun. We can hang around with the tough utilitarian words, like *the*, and have a few beers, or we can wander over and visit the lofty *perambulate*, who turned out to be a very nice verb with a very lovely wife, *tutu*. *Fuzzy* also turned out to be a lot of fun; she had a great sense of humor and a welcoming manner that we all learned from. I can never decide whether I'd like to be pro-letariat or bourgeois in this world of words. The common words, such as the pronouns and the transitive verbs, get used a lot, but they're tired (you should see them running around here, carrying their objects). The exciting words, like *fo'c'sle*, make a lot of impact but aren't frequently called into service. I'm lucky. I'm *underpants*. Sometimes I'm used innocuously, but other times I get to be in very racy sentences in some pretty damn good books. Of course, some usages I find shocking. Which is a point I'd like to make:

When you read something that disgusts you, don't blame the word. *Scrotum* goes around here like someone just shot his best friend, but really he's a legitimate guy who gets used in ugly ways by a lot of cheeseballs. Likewise *pimple*. I was there when he got used as "a pimple on the face of humanity." The poor guy was blue for a month. He walked around here with a hangdog look and even tried to be friends with *hangdog look*, but around here, a phrase won't mingle with a word; they just won't. It also irks me that two ordinary words can be given a hyphen and suddenly they're all-important. Me? Of course I would love to be a proper noun, but I'm not, so that's that. Even with the current fad of giving children unusual names, it's unlikely that any couple will call a newborn *Underpants*.

This is also my first experience being on a page, since my typing on January 23 (birthday coming up!). When I was a computer word, things were great. I could blast through cyberspace, scroll across screens, travel to India. Now that I'm on the page, I'm worried that it's going to be mostly dark. My request to you, the person above me, with the two gigantic lenses over your eyes, is that you occasionally open the book after you have finished reading it and give all of us a little air. A simple thumbing through will do. Not that I'm unhappy in here. There are enough diverse words that our little civilization can keep itself amused for the twenty or so years we expect to be on a shelf, or stacked in a corner, or sold in a garage.

I'd also like to say something to you budding writers. Believe me, I do understand that sometimes it's essential to use incorrect grammar. That is fine with me, and the words who are in those sentences are aware of their lot in life. But it's difficult to even hang around an incomplete sentence, much less be in one. I imagine it's like talking to a person whose head is missing. It just doesn't feel right. A friend of mine has been misspelled in a computer file for over fourteen years, and it doesn't look like he's ever going to be spellchecked.

There are a couple of individuals who would like to speak:

> I'm the word *sidle*, and it was fun to be in that story about the dog (I couldn't see the title from where I was).

> Greetings. I'm *scummy*, and I'd like to mention that you are a lowlife.

> Hello. I'm *hello*, and I'd like to say myself.

And now we'd like to hear from a group of individuals without whom none of the work we do would be possible:

> Hi. We're the letters, and we'd just like to say that we enjoy being a part of the very fine words on this page. Thank you.

And last but not least, someone very special to the whole crew here in *Pure Drivel* would like to end this book:

?

from *Pure Drivel*

RICHARD WILBUR

The Writer

In her room at the prow of the house
Where light breaks, and the windows are tossed with linden,
My daughter is writing a story.

I pause in the stairwell, hearing
From her shut door a commotion of typewriter-keys
Like a chain hauled over a gunwale.

Young as she is, the stuff
Of her life is a great cargo, and some of it heavy:
I wish her a lucky passage.

But now it is she who pauses,
As if to reject my thought and its easy figure.
A stillness greatens, in which

The whole house seems to be thinking,
And then she is at it again with a bunched clamor
Of strokes, and again is silent.

I remember the dazed starling
Which was trapped in that very room, two years ago;
How we stole in, lifted a sash

And retreated, not to affright it;
And how for a helpless hour, through the crack of the door,
We watched the sleek, wild, dark

And iridescent creature
Batter against the brilliance, drop like a glove
To the hard floor, or the desk-top,

And wait then, humped and bloody,
For the wits to try it again; and how our spirits
Rose when, suddenly sure,

It lifted off from a chair-back,
Beating a smooth course for the right window
And clearing the sill of the world.

It is always a matter, my darling,
Of life and death, as I had forgotten. I wish
What I wished you before, but harder.

FRAN LEBOWITZ

꧁

Writing: A Life Sentence

Contrary to what many of you might imagine, a career in letters is not without its drawbacks — chief among them the unpleasant fact that one is frequently called upon to actually sit down and write. This demand is peculiar to the profession and, as such, galling, for it is a constant reminder to the writer that he is not now, nor will he ever really be, like other men. For the requirements of the trade are so unattractive, so not fair, and so foreign to regular people that the writer is to the real world what Esperanto is to the language world — funny, maybe, but not *that* funny. This being the case, I feel the time has come for all concerned to accept the writer's differences as inherent and acknowledge once and for all that in the land of the blind the one-eyed man is a writer and he's not too thrilled about it.

Thus I offer the following with the hope that it will bring about much-needed compassion. Points 1 through 5 are for parents — the later explication for masochists. Or vice versa.

How to Tell if Your Child Is a Writer

Your child is a writer if one or more of the following statements are applicable. Truthfulness is advised — no amount of fudging will alter the grim reality.

1. Prenatal
   A. You have morning sickness at night because the fetus finds it too distracting to work during the day.
   B. You develop a craving for answering services and typists.
   C. When your obstetrician applies his stethoscope to your abdomen he hears excuses.

2. Birth
   A. The baby is at least three weeks late because he had a lot of trouble with the ending.
   B. You are in labor for twenty-seven hours because the baby left everything until the last minute and spent an inordinate amount of time trying to grow his toes in a more interesting order.
   C. When the doctor spanks the baby the baby is not at all surprised.
   D. It is definitely a single birth because the baby has dismissed being twins as too obvious.

3. Infancy
   A. The baby refuses both breast and bottle, preferring instead Perrier with a twist in preparation for giving up drinking.
   B. The baby sleeps through the night almost immediately. Also through the day.
   C. The baby's first words, uttered at the age of four days, are "Next week."
   D. The baby uses teething as an excuse not to learn to gurgle.
   E. The baby sucks his forefinger out of a firm conviction that the thumb's been done to death.

4. Toddlerhood
   A. He rejects teddy bears as derivative.
   B. He arranges his alphabet blocks so as to spell out derisive puns on the names of others.
   C. When he is lonely he does not ask his mother for a baby brother or sister but rather for a protégé.
   D. When he reaches the age of three he considers himself a trilogy.
   E. His mother is afraid to remove his crayoned handiwork from the living room walls lest she be accused of excessive editing.
   F. When he is read his bedtime story he makes sarcastic remarks about style.

5. Childhood
   A. At age seven he begins to think about changing his name. Also his sex.
   B. He balks at going to summer camp because he is aware that there may be children there who have never heard of him.
   C. He tells his teachers that he didn't do his homework because he was blocked.
   D. He refuses to learn how to write a Friendly Letter because he knows he never will.
   E. With an eye to a possible movie deal, he insists upon changing the title of his composition "What I Did on My Summer Vacation" to the far snappier "Vacation."
   F. He is thoroughly hypochondriac and is convinced that his chicken pox is really leprosy.
   G. On Halloween he goes out trick-or-treating dressed as Harold Acton.

By the time this unfortunate child has reached puberty there is no longer any hope that he will outgrow being a writer and become something more appealing — like a kidnap victim. The concern, then, as he enters the difficult period of adolescence, is that he receive the proper education in a sympathetic environment. For this reason it is strongly recommended that the teen writer attend a school geared to his dilemma — Writing High. At Writing High the student will be among his own kind — the ungrateful. He will be offered a broad range of subjects relevant to his needs: Beginning Badly, Avoiding Los Angeles One and Too, Remedial Wakefulness, Magazine Editors: Why?, and Advanced Deftness of Phrase — all taught by jealous teachers who would really rather be students. Extracurricular activities (such as the Jacket Flap Club, where students have fun while learning the rudiments of acquiring colorful temporary jobs such as lumberjack, numbers runner, shepherd, and pornographer) are in plentiful supply. The figure of speech team, the Metaphors, are mighty effective. They can mix it up with the best of them, and Janet Flanner, their lovable mascot, is a great campus favorite.

Although the yearbook — *The Contempt* — is rarely finished in time for graduation, it is nevertheless a treasured memento of the years spent at Writing High. The cafeteria is presided over by an overweight woman of great ambition and serves mediocre Italian food at ridiculously inflated prices. School spirit is encouraged by holding in the auditorium a weekly gathering known as Asimile. Tutoring is available for the slow student, or "ghost," as he is referred to at Writing High. Upon graduation or expulsion (and expulsion is favored by the more commercial students, who prize it for its terrific possibilities as a talk-show anecdote) the writer is as ready as he'll ever be to make his mark upon the world.

It is unnecessary to detail the next, or actual career, stage, for all writers end up the same — either dead or in Homes for the Aged Writer. The prospect of being put in such an establishment is viewed by all writers with great dread and not without reason. Recent scandals have revealed the shockingly widespread sadistic practice of slipping the aged writer unfavorable reviews, and more than one such victim has been found dead from lack of sufficient praise.

Not a very pretty picture, I'm afraid, and not a very accurate one either. But don't be encouraged by *that* — two wrongs don't make you write.

Sign Writing

November 21, 1994

For people who make their living as writers, the routine messages of everyday life have to be put together with some care. You don't want to leave rough drafts lying around. I've known novelists for whom the prospect of composing a note asking that a son or daughter be excused from gym that day can bring on a serious case of writer's block.

I was reminded of that recently when our car had to be left on city streets for a few days, and I, attempting to benefit from the experience of a couple of trips in the past to A A A A Aardvark Auto-Glass Repair, took on the task of composing a sign to inform potential pillagers that it contained nothing of value. Hours later, my wife happened to ask me to do some little chore around the house and I heard myself saying, "I can't right now. I'm on the fourth draft of this car sign."

There was no reason for her to be surprised. She has seen me stuck badly on an RSVP. In fact, routine social communication can be particularly knotty for writers, since they habitually try to express themselves in ways that are not overused. This is why a biographer who seems capable of producing a 1,200-page volume in fairly short order can often be inexcusably late with, say, a simple thank-you note.

Reading over what he's put on paper, he'll say to himself, "I can't believe that I wrote anything as lame as 'Thanks for a wonderful weekend.'" Then he'll put aside the entire project until a more original phrase comes to him. A few weeks later, while the draft is still marinating on the writer's desk, the weekend's hostess feels confirmed in her impression — an impression that began to surface with the wine-spilling incident on Saturday night — that the biographer is a boor or a yahoo.

What my fourth draft of the car sign said was "No Radio." I thought that was spare and to the point, without extraneous language I came to it from "No Radio or Any Other Valuables," which I decided, after some reflection, protested too much.

"What do you think?" I asked my wife, handing her the sign.

"It's O.K.," my wife said. "I saw some ready-made signs for car windows at the hardware store, and that's what one of them said, so I guess it's what people think is effective."

"You saw the same sign, worded in just that way?"

"I'm not saying you plagiarized it from the hardware store."

"Actually, I haven't been in there in some time," I said.

"It's really O.K.," my wife said. "'No Radio' is fine."

It's fine if you're satisfied to be writing at the same level as some gorilla at the sign factory. Thinking I needed some fresh ideas, I phoned my older daughter, who lives just around the corner. "What would be a good sign to put in the car to discourage crackheads from smashing the window so they can get at six cents in change on the floor and the spare fan belt and an old pair of pliers?" I asked.

My daughter, a survivor of one of those earnest and progressive nursery schools in Greenwich Village, said, "How about 'Use Words Not Hands'?"

This was a reference to what the teachers at her nursery school were constantly saying as the little monsters attacked one another with any weapon at hand. At one point we all began to wonder exactly what the words for sneaking up behind another kid and pulling her hair might be.

It wouldn't surprise me at all if that hair-puller had turned to a life of petty crime. As much as I enjoyed contemplating the look on his face when he spotted his nursery-school slogan on a car he was about to break into, I decided that the impact of "Use Words Not Hands" rested on the sort of allusion that an editor would criticize as "too inside."

The next draft was a complete departure — more of a new approach, really, than another draft. It said, "There Is Nothing of Value Here." Upon reflection, I decided that it sounded too philosophical. I could picture a car thief who came upon it turning to his partner in crime and saying, "Talk about pretentious!"

So now I'm sort of stuck. Meanwhile, the car's on the street. It is not completely without protection. An old shirt cardboard taped onto the backseat window bears the words "Sign in Preparation."

SOME THIN LINE
OF COMFORT

We all know that books burn — but we have the greater knowledge that books cannot be killed by fire.

Franklin D. Roosevelt

Remember
First to possess his books; for without them
He's but a sot, as I am, nor hath not
One Spirit to command: they all do hate him
As rootedly as I. Burn but his books.

William Shakespeare
THE TEMPEST

Knowledge unfits a child to be a slave.

Frederick Douglass

Discovery is not change. To discover is to stand before the bridge that leads to change.

Dr. Richard Firestone

✦►─►►─◄─◄─◄✦

ALBERTO MANGUEL

A History of Reading

I first kept my books in straight alphabetical order, by author. Then I began dividing them by genre: novels, essays, plays, poems. Later on I tried grouping them by language, and when, during the course of my travels, I was obliged to keep only a few, I separated them into those I hardly ever read, those I read all the time and those I was hoping to read. Sometimes my library obeyed secret rules, born from idiosyncratic associations. The Spanish novelist Jorge Semprún kept Thomas Mann's *Lotte in Weimar* among his books on Buchenwald, the concentration camp in which he had been interned, because the novel opens with a scene at Weimar's Elephant Hotel, where Semprún was taken after his liberation. Once I thought it would be amusing to construct from such groupings a history of literature, exploring, for instance, the relationships between Aristotle, Auden, Jane Austen and Marcel Aymé (in my alphabetical order), or between Chesterton, Sylvia Townsend Warner, Borges, Saint John of the Cross and Lewis Carroll (among those I most enjoy). It seemed to me that the literature taught at school — in which links were explained between Cervantes and Lope de Vega based on the fact that they shared a century, and in which Juan Ramón Jiménez's *Platero y yo* (a purple tale of a poet's infatuation with a donkey) was considered a masterpiece — was as arbitrary or as permissible a selection as the literature I could construct myself, based on my findings along the crooked road of my own readings and the size of my own bookshelves. The history of literature, as consecrated in school manuals and official libraries, appeared to me to be nothing more than the history of certain readings — albeit older and better informed than mine, but no less dependent on chance and on circumstance.

One year before graduating from high school, in 1966, when the military government of General Onganía came to power, I discovered yet another system by which a reader's books can be arranged. Under suspicion of being Communist or obscene, certain titles and certain authors were placed on the censor's list, and in the ever-increasing police checks in cafés, bars and train stations, or simply on the street, it became as important not to be seen with a suspicious book in hand as it was to carry proper identification. The banned authors — Pablo Neruda, J. D. Salinger, Maxim Gorky, Harold Pinter — formed another, different history of literature, whose links were neither evident nor everlasting, and whose communality was revealed exclusively by the punctilious eye of the censor.

But not only totalitarian governments fear reading. Readers are bullied in schoolyards and in locker-rooms as much as in government offices and prisons. Almost everywhere, the community of readers has an ambiguous reputation that comes from its acquired authority and perceived power. Something in the relationship between a reader and a book is recognized as wise and fruitful, but it is also seen as disdainfully exclusive and excluding, perhaps because the image of an individual curled up in a corner, seemingly oblivious of the grumblings of the world, suggests impenetrable privacy and a selfish eye and singular secretive action. ("Go out and live!" my mother would say when she saw me reading, as if my silent activity contradicted her sense of what it meant to be alive.) The popular fear of what a reader might do among the pages of a book is like the ageless fear men have of what women might do in the secret places of their body, and of what witches and alchemists might do in the dark behind locked doors. Ivory, according to Virgil, is the material out of which the Gate of False Dreams is made; according to Sainte-Beuve, it is also the material out of which is made the reader's tower.

Learning to Read

Very soon the Yankee teachers
    Came down and set up school;
But, oh! how the Rebs did hate it, —
    It was agin' their rule.

Our masters always tried to hide
    Book learning from our eyes;
Knowledge didn't agree with slavery —
    'Twould make us all too wise.

But some of us would try to steal
    A little from the book,
And put the words together,
    And learn by hook or crook.

I remember Uncle Caldwell,
    Who took pot liquor fat
And greased the pages of his book,
    And hid it in his hat

And had his master ever seen
    The leaves upon his head,
He'd have thought them greasy papers,
    But nothing to be read.

And there was Mr. Turner's Ben,
    Who heard the children spell,

And picked the words right up by heart,
    And learned to read 'em well.

Well the Northern folks kept sending
    The Yankee teachers down;
And they stood right up and helped us,
    Though Rebs did sneer and frown.

And, I longed to read my Bible,
    For precious words it said;
But when I begun to learn it,
    Folks just shook their heads,

And said there is no use trying,
    Oh! Chloe, you're too late;
But as I was rising sixty,
    I had no time to wait.

So I got a pair of glasses,
    And straight to work I went,
And never stopped till I could read
    The hymns and Testament.

Then I got a little cabin
    A place to call my own —
And I felt as independent
    As the queen upon her throne.

Because of Libraries
We Can Say These Things

She is holding the book close to her body,
carrying it home on the cracked sidewalk,
down the tangled hill.
If a dog runs at her again, she will use the book as a shield.

She looked hard among the long lines
of books to find this one.
When they start talking about money,
when the day contains such long and hot places,
she will go inside.
An orange bed is waiting.
Story without corners.
She will have two families.
They will eat at different hours.

She is carrying a book past the fire station
and the five-and-dime.
What this town has not given her
the book will provide; a sheep,
a wilderness of new solutions.
The book has already lived through its troubles.
The book has a calm cover, a straight spine.

When the step returns to itself
as the best place for sitting,

and the old men up and down the street
are latching their clippers,

she will not be alone.
She will have a book to open
and open and open.
Her life starts here.

AUDRE LORDE

❧

Story Books on a Kitchen Table

Out of her womb of pain my mother spat me
into her ill-fitting harness of despair
into her deceits
where anger re-conceived me
piercing my eyes like arrows
pointed by her nightmare
of who I was not
becoming.

Going away
she left in her place
iron maidens to protect me
and for my food
the wrinkled milk of legend
where I wandered through the lonely rooms of afternoon
wrapped in nightmares
from the Orange and Red and Yellow
Purple and Blue and Green
Fairy Books
where White witches ruled
over the empty kitchen table
and never wept
or offered gold
nor any kind enchantment
for the vanished mother
of a black girl.

ANNE CASTON

The Book

On a give-away table at the library when I was twelve:
gold-embossed letters on a black cloth cover.
I took it to the librarian who drew a line of little *xxx*s
through the library name and stamped
"This book belongs to _____" in the front cover.
She watched as I penciled my name in the space.
She initialed it and handed it back to me.
So it came to be my book.

When I asked my father later if it was true,
what the book said, he told me, *Girl, you can't
believe everything you read in books,*
and he went back to work on his model planes.

So I asked my teacher about it too.
She *said, Well, yes, it's true,
for the most part. It was terrible
but, after all, they killed Christ, the Jews.*

So I hid the book. I put it in a drawer, under my socks,
and late at night while the household slept, I crept
        out of bed
and sat at the moonlit window and turned the pages.

I let myself look at their faces,
their bony arms and legs, the barns of hair,
the little scoops of gold waiting on scales.
One page I returned to every night:
a girl who could've been my age walking, head down,
by a woman's side, carrying a book under her arm.

Just ahead of them, to the side of the gate
they will pass through: a pile,
already burning.

MIGUEL DE CERVANTES

✥

Don Quijote

Don Quijote's niece worries about her uncle:

"These damned books of chivalry that he's always reading have ruined his judgment. And now I recall having heard him say many times, talking to himself, that he wanted to become a roaming knight and seek adventures across the wide world. The devil take those books because, just like that, they've corrupted the most delicate mind in all of La Mancha. . . .

"Many times it happened that my noble uncle would read one of those soulless books of misadventures for two days and nights, after which he'd throw down the book, pick up his sword, and slash away at the walls. And when he was tired, he'd say he'd cut down four giants like four towers. And the sweat of exhaustion he sweated, he'd say that was the blood of his battle wounds. . . .

"But I'm to blame for everything because I didn't tell you gentlemen about my uncle's outrageous behavior so you could do something about it before it got to where it got, and could have burnt all those cursed books. Because he has many books that deserve to be burnt as if they were heretics. . . ."

So, while Quijote slept, the priest asked the niece for the keys to the room where the dangerous books were kept and she gladly gave them to him. They went in, along with the housekeeper, and found more than a hundred heavy volumes, very well bound, and other smaller ones. As soon as the housekeeper saw the books, she quickly ran out of the storeroom and resumed with a bowl of holy water and a handful of purifying plants and said, "Take this, your worship, Mister Priest. Sprinkle this room in case there's some spirit here from the many that are in these books. They might curse us for the harm we're about to do them by throwing them out of this world."

The priest laughed at the housekeeper's simplicity and asked to be handed the books one by one so he could see what they were about, because he might discover some which didn't deserve to go up in flames.

"No," said the niece, "we mustn't spare a single one because they've all been damaging. It will be better to throw them out the windows into the courtyard, make a pile of them, and set them on fire or take them to the back yard and make a bonfire there so the smoke won't bother us."

The housekeeper said the same, such was the desire of the two of them for the death of those innocents, but the priest would not agree without at least reading the titles first. . . .

That night the housekeeper burned all the books in the courtyard and all those in the house, and many of those burnt were of such quality that they deserved to be kept in perpetual archives. But bad luck and the laziness of the inquisitor never allowed it. And so these people proved the old refrain that sometimes the saints pay for the sinners.

Translated from the Castilian by Rob Ackerman

➤➤ BIBLIOPHILE ◄◄

→→ THE COMMON READER ←←

MAXINE KUMIN

⁂

On Reading an Old Baedeker in
Schloss Leopoldskron

Salzburg, Austria

Soft as beetpulp, the cover
of this ancient Baedeker.
The gold print has scabbed off the leather
but thirty-three tissue paper maps extend
from Vienna to Bosnia. One
of my grandfathers is in here somewhere
living in three rooms over his tailor
shop on the Judengasse in Salzburg or
Prague, stitching up frock coats on Jew
Alley in Pilsen, or in the mews
of Vienna's Old Quarter,
my mother's loyal obsequious *Opa*
tugging his forelock whenever
the name of Franz Joseph is spoken.

In this edition you can still travel
by diligence down from Bad Ischl
to Hallstatt, where grottoes full of bones
of early Celt miners have been uncovered.
Whole families journey to see them
cycling single file, observing the caution
to keep to the left "because in
whatever part of the Empire you meet them,

troops on the march, sized by height
and moving smartly, always keep right."

Not for you, *Opa*, this tourist attraction,
punts lapping the stone-green lake in
the hanging valley of Hallstatt,
languorous voices hovering
adrift in dappled sunlight
and the Lionel-toy train tunneling
out of its papier-mâché mountain
to pause at the cardboard station
where day trippers, disembarking,
may visit the fake antique ruin,
a mossed-over stucco *folly*.
Time to shoulder your knapsack
and strike out for Ellis Island.
Kiss you nine sisters and never look back.

Never look back, Grandfather.
Don't catch my eye on this marble
staircase as wide as the 'gasse
you lived in. Don't look at the chandeliers
that shone on the Nazi Gauleiter
who moved in and made this headquarters.
Here in the cavernous Great Hall
I look for some thin line of comfort
that binds us, some weight-bearing bridge

and finally walk out in rain
to fling stale rolls to the swans
in their ninetieth generation.

Lives of the Nineteenth-Century Poetesses

As girls they were awkward and peculiar,
wept in church or refused to go at all.
Their mothers saw right away no man would marry them.
So they must live at the sufferance of others,
timid and queer as governesses out of Chekhov,
malnourished on theology, boiled eggs, and tea,
but given to outbursts of pride that embarrass everyone.
After the final quarrel, the grand
renunciation, they retire upstairs to the attic
or to the small room in the cheap off-season hotel
and write *Today I burned all your letters* or
I dreamed the magnolia blazed like an avenging angel
and when I woke I knew I was in Hell.
No one is surprised when they die young,
having left all their savings to a wastrel nephew,
to be remembered for a handful
of "minor but perfect" lyrics,
a passion for jam or charades,
and a letter still preserved in the family archives:
"I send you herewith the papers of your aunt
who died last Tuesday in the odor of sanctity
although a little troubled in her mind
by her habit, much disapproved of by the ignorant,
of writing down the secrets of her heart."

KATE RUSHIN

❦

Reading Lists

for Frank D. Rushin

I want
To exchange books with my father
I want to give him *Zami* and *The Bluest Eye*
Member of the Wedding and *The Yearling*

(I want him to ignore The War and the advice
Colored boys need to take up a trade
I want his eyes to be good)

The books I want most to give to my father are
The ones I write
The books I want most to read are
The ones he would have written

Union Station Atlanta 1939 Ten Cents A Bag
How I Got Busted Down In This White Man's
Army And Worked My Way Up Again
How I Put It All On The Shelf
And Kept On Doing What I Needed To Do

GEOFFREY O'BRIEN

~❧~

Prisoners

The horror would be to have read all that was written, to
have come to the end of books: a horror that prisoners and
soldiers know, parceling out their few available books page
by page, a page a day so as to last out the year. The American taken prisoner by the Germans was told that he would
he given one book a week, selected at random by his jailers:
the world would be heaven or hell depending on whether
the book was a novel by John Galsworthy or a manual of
chemical elements, the life of Julian the Apostate or a direc-
tory of the Shriners of Luzerne County, Pennsylvania.

The prisoner in Stefan Zweig's *The Royal Game* saw sal-
vation from his solitary imprisonment by the Gestapo in the
book he was able to smuggle into his cell, without having any
idea of its nature until he was finally alone with his prize:

> *The mere idea of a book in which words appear in orderly
> arrangement, of sentences, pages, leaves, a book in which
> one could follow and stow in one's brain new, unknown,
> diverting thoughts was at once intoxicating and stupefy-
> ing. . . . I wanted, first of all, to savour the joy of possess-
> ing a book; the artificially prolonged and nerve-inflaming
> desire to day-dream about the kind of book I would wish
> this stolen one to be.*

It turned out, to his initial horror, to be an anthology of
chess games: something that could not be read at all with-

out mastering a hitherto alien language. Through absorption in those diagrams, the prisoner would in the end explore the outer limits of monomania, literally driven mad by his involuntary choice of reading matter.

I prefer to believe that somewhere in this heap of books there is one I cannot imagine. The unread book is the life yet to be lived, the promise that there will be new ideas, images never yet glimpsed. The paradise of futurity is the thousand page book full of episodes still to come: a book of mysteries disguised as a mystery book with an inexplicably alluring title, *The Secret of the Desert* or *The Adventure of the Lost Key*.

VIKRAM SETH

❧

Poet

for Irina Ratushinskaya

She lived for six years in a cage. When I
Am inclined to regret the way things are, I think
Of her who through long cold and pain did not
Betray the ones she loved or plead for mercy.
They censored the few letters they allowed.
Cabbage and bread, rotten and stale, were food.
While outside governments and springs went round
And summits, thaws, and great events occurred,
Here inside was no hope. Years of her youth
Were sickened for no crime. She did not even
Know if her lover knew she was alive.
The paper she'd written poems on was removed.
What could she find? — the swirls in the cold blue light
Through bars so thick her hands could not pass through
    them —
Those swirls of blue light and the heels of bread
She shared with some companionable mouse.
Her poems she memorized line by line and destroyed.
The Contents were what was difficult to remember.

CZESLAW MILOSZ

And Yet the Books

And yet the books will be there on the shelves, separate
    beings,
That appeared once, still wet
As shining chestnuts under a tree in autumn,
And, touched, coddled, began to live
In spite of fires on the horizon, castles blown up,
Tribes on the march, planets in motion.
"We are," they said, even as their pages
Were being torn out, or a buzzing flame
Licked away their letters. So much more durable
Than we are, who frail warmth
Cools down with memory, disperses, perishes.
I imagine the earth when I am no more:
Nothing happens, no loss, it's still a strange pageant,
Women's dresses, dewy lilacs, a song in the valley.
Yet the books will be there on the shelves, well born,
Derived from people, but also from radiance, heights.

WHERE BOOKS
FALL OPEN

-+>-+>-<+-<+-

Only in books has mankind known perfect truth,
love and beauty.

George Bernard Shaw

Science, seeking confirmation, proof, objective testing
and proof, cannot avail itself of this cardinal human
loneliness, but literature can. And this with language
that is always failing and stumbling, breaking the writer's
heart with its mere appropriateness to the thing in his
mind. . . . Science progresses all the time, literature never.
How should it "improve" over the centuries when
its very subject is the enigma, the inaccessibility
of the human condition?

Alfred Kazin

The true felicity of a lover of books is the luxurious
turning of page by page, the surrender, not meanly abject,
but deliberate and cautious, with your wits about you,
as you deliver yourself into the keeping of the book. . . .
This I call reading.

Edith Wharton

The greatest masterpiece in literature is only
a dictionary out of order.

Jean Cocteau

-+>-+>-<+-<+-

JAMES SEAY

Where Books Fall Open

It was not solely to test its heft
that I took the book's spine in my palm
and gave that slight downward gesture,
then let it rest;
rather it was in the way one calm
with the newborn will lift
an infant and do the same.
A way of welcome,
perhaps, but also maybe ritual
born of hope in what is gathered
there in signatures or swaddle.
At any rate, the book at hand
fell open to "Snow-Bound",
Whittier's once-famous *winter idyl*
to what he called *the chill embargo*
of the snow, a week or so in his youth
when all the world he would know
was that of barn and hearth.
The thin line of wear along the length
of the book's fore-edge told where
reader after reader returned to hear
again the known measures of that winter storm,
the allure of the pull wombward,
as some might read it,
or the consonance of fire's gold with bourgeois habit,

or comfort of rest in one's assigned quarters
in the old patriarchal orders.
But this is to put too critical a point
on the simple literature of nostalgia.
Easier to accept it as heartfelt
yet innocent of how it gives us
only the no-surprises tour,
the driver of the bus
unloading the seemingly undimmed regalia
of time's little tea party in our honor.
Mais ou sont les neiges d'antan?
I think of where books fall open
to passages that promise that sojourn
at our chosen destination,
how it may be nostalgia's predictable return
or the alternative other, a passage rendering the known
familiar enough but at the same time
altering our sense of it, like *snow falling
faintly through the universe*,
and to follow that passage on out, *faintly
falling . . . upon all the living
and the dead*. Swoon is not too strong a term.
Nor at another time would doubt be —
or any word that tells of the changing dream
we have of the place, and the changing claim.
A final word, though, in the old poet's defense:
he spoke of the traveller who has *the grateful sense
of sweetness near, he knows not whence.*
Where then will our own book fall open,
and with what sweetness of the where we have not been?

ELIZABETH HARDWICK

✵

On Reading

As I have grown older I see myself as fortunate in many ways. It is fortunate to have had all my life this passion for studying and enjoying literature and for trying to add a bit to it as interestingly as I can. This passion has given me much joy, it has given me friends who care for the same things, it has given me employment, escape from boredom, everything. The greatest gift is the passion for reading. It is cheap, it consoles, it distracts, it excites, it gives you knowledge of the world and experience of a wide kind. It is a moral illumination.

VIRGINIA WOOLF

❧

The Common Reader

There is a sentence in Dr. Johnson's Life of Gray which
might well be written up in all those rooms, too humble
to be called libraries, yet full of books, where the pursuit
of reading is carried on by private people. "...I rejoice to
concur with the common reader; for by the common sense
of readers, uncorrupted by literary prejudices, after all the
refinements of subtilty and the dogmatism of learning,
must be finally decided all claim to poetical honours." It
defines their qualities; it dignifies their aims; it bestows
upon a pursuit which devours a great deal of time, and is
yet apt to leave behind it nothing very substantial, the sanc-
tion of the great man's approval.

The common reader, as Dr. Johnson implies, differs from
the critic and the scholar. He is worse educated, and nature
has not gifted him so generously. He reads for his own pleas-
ure rather than to impart knowledge or correct the opinions
of others. Above all, he is guided by an instinct to create for
himself, out of whatever odds and ends he can come by,
some kind of whole — a portrait of a man, a sketch of an
age, a theory of the art of writing. He never ceases, as he
reads, to run up some rickety and ramshackle fabric which
shall give him the temporary satisfaction of looking suffi-
ciently like the real object to allow of affection, laughter, and
argument. Hasty, inaccurate, and superficial, snatching now
this poem, now that scrap of old furniture without caring

where he finds it or of what nature it may be so long as it serves his purpose and rounds his structure, his deficiencies as a critic are too obvious to be pointed out; but if he has, as Dr. Johnson maintained, some say in the final distribution of poetical honours, then, perhaps, it may be worth while to write down a few of the ideas and opinions which, insignificant in themselves, yet contribute to so mighty a result.

MARIANNE MOORE

Poetry

I, too, dislike it.
    Reading it, however, with a perfect contempt for it, one
                                             discovers in
   it, after all, a place for the genuine.

→→ JAMES AT 12 ←←

➵ ELIZABETH AND EMME ➴

RACHEL HADAS

Teaching Emily Dickinson

What starts as one more Monday morning class
merges to a collective Dickinson,
separate vessels pooling some huge truth
sampled bit by bit by each of us.

She sings the pain of loneliness for one.
Another sees a life of wasted youth;
then one long flinching from what lay beneath
green earth; last, pallid peerings at the stone

she too now knows the secret of.

                Alone,
together, we'd decipher BIRD SOUL BEE
dialect humdrum only until heard
with the rapt nervy patience, Emily,
you showed us that we owed you. One small bird
opens its wings. They spread. They cover us:
myriad lives foreshortened into Word.

ROBERT PINSKY

Library Scene

TO P.S.

Under the ceiling of metal stamped like plaster
And below the ceiling fan, in the brown luster

Someone is reading, in the sleepy room
Alert, her damp cheek balanced on one palm,

With knuckles loosely holding back the pages
Or fingers waiting lightly at their edges.

Her eyes are like the eyes of someone attending
To a fragile work, familiar and demanding —

Some work of delicate surfaces or threads.
Someone is reading the way a rare child reads,

A kind of changeling reading for love of reading,
For love and for the course of something leading

Her child's intelligent soul through its inflection:
A force, a kind of loving work or action.

Someone is reading in a deepening room
Where something happens, something that will come

To happen again, happening as many times
As she is reading in as many rooms.

What happens outside that calm like water braiding
Over green stones? The ones of little reading

Or who never read for love, are many places.
They are in the house of power, and many houses

Reading as they do, doing what they do.
Or it happens that they come, at times, to you

Because you are somehow someone that they need:
They come to you and you tell them how you read.

Love in the Valley

The sun goes slowly blind.
It is this mountain, shrouding
the valley of the shadow,

widening like amnesia
evening dims the mind.
I shake my head in darkness,

it is a tree branched with cries,
a trash can full of print.
Now, through the reddening squint

of leaves leaden as eyes,
a skein of drifting hair
like a twig fallen on snow

branches the blank pages.
I bring it close, and stare
in slow vertiginous darkness,

and now I drift elsewhere,
through hostile images
of white and black, and look,

like a thaw-sniffing stallion, the head
of Pasternak emerges with its forelock,
his sinewy wrist a fetlock

pawing the frozen spring,
till his own hand has frozen
on the white page, heavy.

I ride through a white childhood
whose pines glittered with bracelets,
when I heard wolves, feared the black wood,

every wrist-aching brook
and the ice maiden
in Hawthorne's fairy book.

The hair melts into dark,
a question mark that led
where the untethered mind

strayed from its first track;
now Hardy's sombre head
upon which hailstorms broke

looms, like a weeping rock,
like wind, the tresses drift
and their familiar trace

tingles across the face
with light lashes.
I knew the depth of whiteness,

I feared the numbing kiss
of those women of winter,
Bathsheba, Lara, Tess,

whose tragedy made less
of life, whose love was more
than love of literature.

JANE AUSTEN

✻

Northanger Abbey

"What are you reading, Miss ——— ?" "Oh! It's only a novel!" replies the young lady; while she lays down her book with affected indifference, or momentary shame. "It is only *Cecilia*, or *Camilla*, or *Belinda*"; or, in short, only some work in which the greatest powers of the mind are displayed; in which the most thorough knowledge of human nature, the happiest delineation of its varieties, the liveliest effusions of wit or humour, are conveyed to the world in the best chosen language.

CAROL WESTON

Becoming a Reader

When I was a girl, I didn't read much. I spent evenings playing Kick the Can with my brothers and neighbors. Even at
night, I was too restless to read and was more likely to keep a
diary than open a book. Then I discovered Aesop's fables
and Archie comics, E. B. White and Dear Abby, Roald Dahl
and *True Confessions*. By high school, I was a slow but sure
reader. In college, I was a comparative literature major.

God, it was great when reading was homework. When
my professors said I *had* to read Rabelais, Racine, Rostand,
García Lorca, and García Márquez. When reading was what
was required of me.

Now that I am grown up, life gets in the way of reading.
I try to compensate. At the gym, I'm the one reading while
peddling that bicycle that goes nowhere. I read on buses and
lines, and if a book is really good, I sometimes read while
walking. I always lug novels in my purse; *War and Peace*
weighed me down for months, though I tend toward shorter
fare.

I'm even a member of two book clubs. One is a
women's group that has been meeting for a dozen years; the
other is for mothers and daughters. Both keep me from
becoming one of those misguided souls who claim to be too
busy to read.

What is it about reading?

Books offer life, distilled. They have the power to change minds and change moods.

Books are bridges. If you and I read the same book, we have common ground, ideas and individuals we can discuss.

Books fill the empty spaces. They keep us company. Recently I was far from home — on a book tour, ironically — and I was suddenly lonely. I sat down in Atlanta, ordered coffee for one, opened my purse and — abracadabra — a charming British author joined me. She was eloquent and witty and I didn't even have to hold up my end of the conversation. All I had to do was turn pages. Because I had a book, I was not alone.

What a privilege to know that if I have an extra hour, anywhere, anytime, I can spend it with Edith Wharton or Oscar Wilde. What a comfort that if I want to be with Anna Karenina or Harry Potter, there they are, ready and waiting.

Ah, but here are my *True Confessions*: My nature is still restless; I'm still more likely to be "doing" than sitting; I rarely gobble a book whole, unless felled by the flu. And so, I am not merely comforted, but chagrined, by how many great books (Anna K!) I have yet to read — let alone reread.

Perhaps when I am older, my daughters grown, my deadlines met, my life less distracting, I will read more. Perhaps I will sit, contented, with a book, a glass of sherry, and a cat. Maybe two cats.

When I was a girl, I didn't read much.

I still don't read enough.

But chapter by chapter, book by book, I am catching up.

RITA DOVE

❧

Maple Valley Branch Library, 1967

For a fifteen-year-old there was plenty
to do: Browse the magazines,
slip into the Adult Section to see
what vast *tristesse* was born of rush-hour traffic,
décolletés, and the plague of too much money.
There was so much to discover — how to
lay out a road, the language of flowers,
and the place of women in the tribe of Moost.
There were equations elegant as a French twist,
fractal geometry's unwinding maple leaf;

I could follow, step-by-step, the slow disclosure
of a pineapple Jell-O mold — or take
the path of Harold's purple crayon through
the bedroom window and onto a lavender
spill of stars. Oh, I could walk any aisle
and smell wisdom, put a hand out to touch
the rough curve of bound leather,
the harsh parchment of dreams.

As for the improbable librarian
with her salt and paprika upsweep,
her British accent and sweater clip
(mom of a kid I knew from school) —
I'd go up to her desk and ask for help
on bareback rodeo or binary codes,

phonics, Gestalt theory,
lead poisoning in the Late Roman Empire,
the play of light in Dutch Renaissance painting;
I would claim to be researching
pre-Columbian pottery or Chinese foot-binding,
but all I wanted to know was:
Tell me what you've read that keeps
that half smile afloat
above the collar of your impeccable blouse.

So I read *Gone with the Wind* because
it was big, and haiku because they were small.
I studied history for its rhapsody of dates,
lingered over Cubist art for the way
it showed all sides of a guitar at once.
All the time in the world was there, and sometimes
all the world on a single page.
As much as I could hold
on my plastic card's imprint I took,

greedily: six books, six volumes of bliss,
the stuff we humans are made of:
words and sighs and silence,
ink and whips, Brahma and cosine,
corsets and poetry and blood sugar levels —
I carried it home, past five blocks of aluminum siding
and the old garage where, on its boarded-up doors,
someone had scrawled:

I CAN EAT AN ELEPHANT
IF I TAKE SMALL BITES.

Yes, I said, to no one in particular: *That's*
what I'm gonna do!

~∗~

Swann's Way

And as I did not wish to interrupt my reading, I would go on with it in the garden, under the chestnut tree, in a hooded chair of wicker and canvas in the depths of which I used to sit and feel that I was hidden from the eyes of anyone who might be coming to call upon the family.

And then my thoughts, too, formed a similar sort of recess, in the depths of which I felt that I could bury myself and remain invisible even while I looked at what went on outside. When I saw an external object, my consciousness that I was seeing it would remain between me and it, surrounding it with a thin spiritual border that prevented me from ever touching its substance directly; for it would somehow evaporate before I could make contact with it, just as an incandescent body that is brought into proximity with something wet never actually touches its moisture, since it is always preceded by a zone of evaporation. Upon the sort of screen dappled with different states and impressions which my consciousness would simultaneously unfold while I was reading, and which ranged from the most deeply hidden aspirations of my heart to the wholly external view of the horizon spread out before my eyes at the bottom of the garden, what was my primary, my innermost impulse, the lever whose incessant movements controlled everything else, was my belief in the philosophic richness and beauty of the book I was reading, and my desire to appropriate them for myself, whatever the book might be.

Children Selecting Books in a Library

With beasts and gods, above, the wall is bright.
The child's head, bent to the book-colored shelves,
Is slow and sidelong and food-gathering,
Moving in blind grace ... Yet from the mural, Care,
The grey-eyed one, fishing the morning mist,
Seizes the baby hero by the hair

And whispers, in the tongue of gods and children,
Words of a doom as ecumenical as dawn
But blanched, like dawn, with dew. The children's cries
Are to men the cries of crickets, dense with warmth
— But dip a finger into Fafnir, taste it,
And all their words are plain as chance and pain.

Their tales are full of sorcerers and ogres
Because their lives are: the capricious infinite
That, like parents, no one has yet escaped
Except by luck or magic; and since strength
And wit are useless, be kind or stupid, wait
Some power's gratitude, the tide of things.

Read meanwhile ... hunt among the shelves, as dogs do,
    grasses,
And find one cure for Everychild's diseases
Beginning: *Once upon a time there was*
A wolf that fed, a mouse that warned, a bear that rode
A boy. Us men, alas! wolves, mice, bears bore.

And yet wolves, mice, bears, children, gods and men
In slow perambulation up and down the shelves
Of the universe are seeking ... who knows except
      themselves?
What some escape to, some escape: if we find Swann's
Way better than our own, and trudge on at the back
Of the north wind to — to — somewhere east
Of the sun, west of the moon, it is because we live

By trading another's sorrow for our own; another's
Impossibilities, still unbelieved in, for our own ...
"I am myself still"? For a little while, forget:
The world's selves cure that short disease, myself,
And we see bending to us, dewy-eyed, the great
CHANGE, dear to all things not to themselves endeared.

Watching the Commuters Read

A man has fallen asleep and looks
As if he's been shot through the heart,

A frothing copy of Louis L'Amour hitting the floor
With a small fluttering argument.

Another is so encumbered by passion,
His lips purse in a kiss

As he mouths out the consonants
Of a particularly emphatic hero.

And nearest me, a girl in spandex has put her diet book
     aside
And is diligently reading her tennis shoes.

Rubbed to a burnished glow on the courts
And lit now by natural light, they are Aladdin's lamps,

However demoted and adjusted for contemporary life.
And, sure enough, through the train window,

Her wishes whizz by in a comic spree —
Swimming pools and rose gardens, chubby red
     convertibles,

Husbands repairing things, children, puppies, even a pony
Who sails lightly through the air

Above a hurdle with a crooked sign
Proclaiming JESUS IS LORD.

No Lazarus, she nevertheless rises
Out of her seat, wincing

Not with pain, but with thinking, to consider
The upcoming town in which the lawns are vast and even.

I see her whole then, a fine large fruit
Wanting to drop off its tree and ripe for the picking

By the neighborhood true crime bookshop
Where a pale, lightly freckled man with hooded eyelids

Patiently waits. Give her a whodunit, I think,
But tell her who's done it.

Give her a big fat chicken of a book
Whose every feathery phrase contains a clue.

For God's sake, distract her from all these houses
Showing their endings to stories never quite selected

Yet dearly paid for, their heaped-up backyards, their
    Big Boy tomato plants
Arthritic with dreaming and frozen in the midst of great
    speed.

In the shaky aisles, a little future bride covets
Her mother's Harlequin romance — not to read it

But because it is flapping, a giant thick-winged moth
Of pages, way above her head.

Its noise interrupts, with a calm and dignified *Om*
Of chaos, the humbler power of the unopened *Hansel*
    and Gretel

She blithely swings from hand to hand as she jumps.
She knows the secret of reading is, after all, possession.

A benign imperialism for those of us
Who rent our hopes and adventures.

The whitened pages of the train window are gritty
With unreadable Braille, sooty as dextrose to the touch.

I place my hands upon them much as Gretel placed hers
Upon the candy that was so nearly her doom.

→→ RYLONA'S VIEW ←←

→→ LOVERS ←←

COLETTE INEZ

❧

Reading Tu Fu, I Wait for My Husband

Sequences, *Autumn*, *Meditations*, Tu Fu.
I read "a hundred years of the saddest news"
and "the forlorn boat, once and for all
tethers my homeward thoughts."

In the halflight of the booth,
thoughts sputter and leap. My fears are cast
to drift on a raft of words.
When will he arrive? Why is he late?
Reasons gather and disband.

Chang-an has dropped off the cliff
of a thousand years into powdery stones.
Stumps of memory grow in a weed-ridden garden.
The beautiful girls do not gather
kingfisher plumes as gifts
in the China of Deng Xiaoping.

Who will write we lived in a glorious age?
Where are the banners of Emperor Wu?
Tatters in the earth and under the stars
of The Seated Ministers
or placed on graves at the Festival of Tombs.

"Chanting, peering into the distance,
in anguish my white hair droops."
So Tu Fu ends his meditations,

the ones he wrote at K'uei-Chou in Seven Sixty-Six,
his second autumn in the region.

After I put the sequences away,
my attention narrows on a mirror image of myself
grown old, white-haired, waiting for my husband.
Suddenly, out of a shadowy corner, he appears
with a story of confusion and delay.
We kiss. It is our twentieth autumn in the city.

WILLIAM STAFFORD

The Trouble with Reading

When a goat likes a book, the whole book is gone,
and the meaning has to go find an author again.
But when we read, it's just print — deciphering,
like frost on a window: we learn the meaning
but lose what the frost is, and all that world
pressed so desperately behind.

So some time let's discover how the ink
feels, to be clutching all that eternity onto
page after page. But maybe it is better not
to know; ignorance, that wide country,
rewards you just to accept it. You plunge;
it holds you. And you have become a rich darkness.

ADRIAN SPRATT

❧

The Vicarious Activity

Words, that sequence of signs, have once again pulled me into their realm. I might be reading a story, a novel, a poem, even a philosophical essay or a review. Here I am, riding a breathing, muscular horse and donning my hat to a stranger. Or I am caught up in the mystery of the "dapple-dawn-drawn falcon" that is Gerard Manley Hopkins' "Windhover." I am in Philip Marlowe's dreary office or listening to Dr. Jung by Lake Maggiore. Or I am on Robin Island with Nelson Mandela, one moment an observer, the next a fellow prisoner, then uneasily a guard. I might not have experienced these things before, but my mind turns out to have them all in it.

While reading, my mind is not just thinking and feeling, but also sensing. It has touch and vision, taste and sound, all of which mediate between my own experiences and the author's invocations. The meeting place of author and reader has no coordinates or clocks, no regulations or video cameras. All of life, imagination and possibility come together here.

I have friends who argue aloud at the books open before them on the desk or winding steadily through the cassette player. They must maintain an alien status in this other world of reading. Not me. I give myself over until something happens to make me stop. I come away feeling the experiences or the justice of the arguments before becoming aware once again of the children playing outside the window and the need to straighten my spine. Only then do my judging faculties step in and start deliberations. Meanwhile, for those minutes or hours of reading, I was inseparable from all of humanity.

XI CHUAN

~❧~

Books

Books should be illuminated by torches,
just as the Incas illuminated their city.

Torches shone on its
woven fabric, pears, gold and silver utensils —

objects that time uses to express itself
from opposition to unity, revealing the secret of fate,

like Hercules and Plato
attracted by the same spring bee.

"All books are the same book,"
pale Mallarmé said with confidence.

All mistakes are the same mistake,
like Ptolemy's research into earth and stars,

his precise calculations
that only led him to absurd conclusions.

Books create a space larger than books.
The life of fire ends in its own flame.

Emperor Qin Shi haunted the library hallway
and Aldous Huxley,

robbed of the past by a fire,
clarified the rest of his life in a single lecture.

I see a rose
covered with dust; what else can death do?

The lofty bookshelves sag
under thousands of sleeping souls.

We live together,
hiding beneath the spirit's torch.

Silence, hopeful —
every time I open a book, a soul is awakened.

A strange woman walks
in a city I've never seen.

A funeral is taking place
in a dusk I've never entered.

Othello's anger, Hamlet's conscience,
Truth spoken at will, muffled bells.

I read a family prophecy.
The pains I've seen are no more than the pains themselves.

History records only a few people's deeds:
The rest is silence.

≈

April 2

What I like about reading in the dark is
you can't see what you're reading
and must imagine verses equal to your longing
and then Keats shows up with "La Belle Dame
Sans Merci" and Yeats wonders whether
"you" will ever be loved for yourself alone
and not your yellow hair
when I was a Columbia freshman
we had to compare those two poems
I wish I were asked to do that today
for I have finally figured it out
but at the time all I could think to say
was both women, the one whose eyes
were shut with kisses four
and the one with yellow hair,
were the same woman, and I knew her

JOSEPHINE JACOBSON

Gentle Reader

Late in the night when I should be asleep
under the city stars in a small room
I read a poet. A poet: not
a versifier. Not a hot-shot
ethic-monger, laying about
him; not a diary of lying
about in cruel cruel beds, crying.
A poet, dangerous and steep.

O God, it peels me, juices me like a press;
this poetry drinks me, eats me, gut and marrow
until I exist in its jester's sorrow,
until my juices feed a savage sight
that runs along the lines, bright
as beasts' eyes. The rubble splays to dust:
city, book, bed, leaving my ear's lust
saying like Molly, yes, yes, yes O yes.

⊱⊰

This Poem

1

This poem is why
I lie down at night
to sleep; it is why
I defecate, read,
and eat sandwiches;
it is why I get
up in the morning;
it is why I breathe.

2

You think (and I know
because you told me)
that poems exist
to *say* things, as you
telephone and I
write letters — as if
this poem practiced
communication.

3

One time this poem
compared itself to
new machinery,
and another time

to a Holstein's cud.
Eight times five times eight
counts three hundred and
twenty syllables.

4

When you require it,
this poem consoles —
the way a mountain
comforts by staying
as it was despite
earthquakes, Presidents,
divorces, and frosts.
Granite continues.

5

This poem informs
the hurt ear wary
of noises, and sings
to the weeping eye.
When the agony
abates itself, one
may appreciate
arbitrary art.

6

This poem is here.
Could it be someplace
else? Every question
is the wrong question.
The only answer
saunters down the page

in its broken lines
strutting and primping.

7
It styles itself not
for the small mirror
of its own regard —
nor even for yours:
to fix appearance;
to model numbers;
to name charity
"the greatest of these."

8
All night this poem
knocks at the closed door
of sleep: "Let me in."
Suppose all poems
contain this poem,
dreaming one knowledge
shaped by the measure
of the body's word.

GEORGE BRADLEY

6 x 10 x ∞

See how the hand reaches of its own accord
To take the volume from the shelf, how it lifts
The lid from off that levelled block of reason

And passes through small aperture into a world,
Lifts it like a trap door in the mind and moves
From one life, worn and circumscribed, peculiar,

Into the general life, an immense atmosphere.
Here is no response, simple of the soul, physic
Compound of metaphysics, broken wafer to make us
    whole.

Aliment is not our element, nor yet antiphony,
And yet mere breath of such an air sets candles
Dancing on the desk to flare on our interior.

Outside, it is any time of day. Outside, night falls.
Engines mutter through the shade, and hours
Rush toward niagaras that are earth's end.

Here, though, distance drifts above a tranquil sea,
And we transform ourselves, become things seen,
Fetching even as starlight, our wink infinite.

[handwritten annotation:] spine tilted chosen like falling like sunlight into the hand — This is how — you chose me ...

A Little Treatise on Ways of Reading

But isn't this, after all, heaven? This island of books where I am free to look at what I like, linger on what I like? I am in full control. The books exist to be played on by my faculties. They cannot evade me, nor can they hold me a moment longer than I want them to.

*If the sentences knew how I had read them...

But there is nothing they can do. Freedom roves at will among the forms of pretending, as if they were a museum of masks and gestures. The reader can do what he likes here. There are styles of reading as there are styles of writing, as many as the reader can invent. Can I enumerate them? I compose a little treatise in my head, resting my eyes for a few moments from all this fine print, these ornamental chapter headings.

1. He can read by letting the eye rove over the shapes of the letters and find patterns in their textures and clusterings, the distinctive fur patterns and topographic markings, so that an extract of Herrick or Melville becomes — even before the eye can make out the words — as recognizable by its grain as a patch of land seen from a helicopter.

2. He can read as if feasting, nourished by the words as by food and drink.

3. As if the words were part of his body, as if the inwardly

sounded syllables literally coursed through him.

4. As if hearing a music not bound by time, in whose phrases he can abide as long as he likes; as if massaged internally by the syllables.

5. As if the text were just now coming into being and he were present at the moment of writing, of pen scratching against paper.

6. As if inside someone else's head, watching the intimate spectacle of that person's thinking, or as if he simply were that person and were now reading over what he had himself written.

7. As if the text were magical, and made unreal things appear and move; as if everything described in it were actually occurring at the moment of reading.

8. As if the words were alive.

9. As if in their natural state the words would have scattered an instant later, like sparrows or water striders, and it was only by chance that their momentary conjunction had been frozen as by a snapshot.

10. As if each word were alive and had a purpose; as if the words danced together in an elaborate and frantic choreography in order to enact a collective message, like cheerleaders or Red Guards spelling out WE'RE NUMBER ONE or THE EAST IS RED; as if the shapes of stanzas and paragraphs evolved from arcane social rituals practiced by the words among themselves; as if by looking at how they grouped themselves on the page you could form some slight idea of what they were thinking. Or as if the text as a whole were a single conscious being, capable of "bristling" or "breathing" or "insinuating."

11. As if the words had literally been kept alive by human

blood; as if they were the end product of a scientific experiment to prolong the human life span by unnatural means; as if this experiment had been conducted on the basis of a scientific theory that words possessed uncanny and unmentionable powers.

12. As if examining a patch of local foliage; as if the words had forced their way out of the earth; as if the text, once above ground, had aged and become overgrown with moss, had been bored into by insects, had grown thin and brittle. As if by gauging the maturity of the text, how far it had gotten from its origin, the reader measured his own span.

13. As if unintended patterns were revealed in scourings, weatherings, erosions.

14. As if the text were mute and communicated through a kind of dumb show.

15. As if the only significant elements were those left out.

→→ READING IN BED ←←

→→ STILL LIFE WITH BROOKLYN BRIDGE ←←

Reading Myself to Sleep

The house is all in darkness except for this corner bedroom
where the lighthouse of a table lamp is guiding
my eyes through the narrow channels of print,

and the only movement in the night is the slight
swirl of curtains, the easy lift and fall of my breathing,
and the flap of pages as they turn in the wind of my hand.

Is there a more gentle way to go into the night
than to follow an endless rope of sentences
and then to slip drowsily under the surface of a page

into the first tentative flicker of a dream,
passing out of the bright precincts of attention
like cigarette smoke passing through a window screen?

All late readers know this sinking feeling of falling
into the liquid of sleep and then rising again
to the call of a voice that you are holding in your hands,

as if pulled from the sea back into a boat
where a discussion is raging on some subject or other,
on Patagonia or Thoroughbreds or the nature of war.

Is there a better method of departure by night
than this quiet bon voyage with an open book,
the sole companion who has come to see you off,

to wave you into the dark waters beyond language?
I can hear the rush and sweep of fallen leaves outside
where the world lies unconscious, and I can feel myself

dissolving, drifting into a story that will never be written,
letting the book slip to the floor where I will find it
in the morning when I surface, wet and streaked with
   daylight.

JORGE LUIS BORGES

Ars Poetica

To gaze at the river made of time and water
And recall that time itself is another river,
To know we cease to be, just like the river,
And that our faces pass away, just like the water.

To feel that waking is another sleep
That dreams it does not sleep and that death,
Which our flesh dreads, is that very death
Of every night, which we call sleep.

To see in the day or in the year a symbol
Of mankind's days and of his years,
To transform the outrage of the years
Into a music, a rumor and a symbol,

To see in death a sleep, and in the sunset
A sad gold, of such is Poetry
Immortal and a pauper. For Poetry
Returns like the dawn and the sunset.

At times in the afternoons a face
Looks at us from the depths of a mirror;
Art must be like that mirror
That reveals to us this face of ours.

They tell how Ulysses, glutted with wonders,
Wept with love to descry his Ithaca

Humble and green. Art is that Ithaca
Of green eternity, not of wonders.

It is also like an endless river
That passes and remains, a mirror for one same
Inconstant Heraclitus, who is the same
And another, like an endless river.

MARK STRAND

The Night, The Porch

To stare at nothing is to learn by heart
What all of us will be swept into, and baring oneself
To the wind is feeling the ungraspable somewhere close by.
Trees can sway or be still. Day or night can be what they
     wish.
What we desire, more than a season or weather, is the
     comfort
Of being strangers, at least to ourselves. This is the crux
Of the matter, which is why even now we seem to be
     waiting
For something whose appearance would be its vanishing —
The sound, say, of a few leaves falling, or just one leaf,
Or less. There is no end to what we can learn. The book
     out there
Tells us as much, and was never written with us in mind.

⇥ *Acknowledgments* ⇤

My deeply felt thanks to the poets and writers in this book
for their brilliant and generous contributions.

This anthology would not have been possible without the
enthusiasm and expertise of David Lehman and Vickie Karp.
Betty Ann Falletta's expert advice was responsible for many
of these selections; I will be indebted to her lifelong for her
introduction to the works of Billy Collins alone. Bernadette
Evangelist has been unfailingly patient in her assistance with
the cover typography and design. Nick Falletta gave the text
his most graceful and astute editorial consideration. Herb
Scher gave me the gift of a morning of photographic research in the New York Public Library's venerable Reading
Room.

Many thanks for the indulgence and good humor of
James Anthony, Elizabeth and Emme Weston Ackerman,
Mary McClean, Michael Avramides, Katka Konecna, Millie
Monelt, Victoria and Mara de Toledo, Nick Falletta and
Emily, Rylona and Rabiya Watson, Mia, Iris, and Florence.
All generously spent hours as models for the paintings, each
adding great personal character and intimacy to these works.

All this would not have been possible without David
Godine's enduring passion for the subject and art of books
and reading and his support for this volume about books
and reading in particular.

And, of course, a most profound thanks to Michael Avramides for his encouragement of my various and sundry
projects. I have had no need of the quiet, well-lit spaces of
the prerequisite artist and writer's colony; he has most lov-
ingly provided it for my daily life.

⤞ *The Paintings* ⤝

Mujer Leyendo, 1997, 34″ x 34″, oil on canvas, Collection of Diana Voigt.

James at 12, 1999, 34″ x 34″, oil on canvas, Private Collection.

Bibliophile, 1999, 30″ x 48″, oil on canvas, Private Collection.

Library, 2000, 40″ x 40″, oil on canvas, Courtesy of Uptown Gallery.

Reading in Bed, 1994, 34″ x 34″, oil on canvas, Collection of Sara and Richard Rosenstock.

Elizabeth and Emme, 2000, 34″ x 34″, oil on canvas, Collection of Carol Weston and Robert Ackerman.

Still Life with Brooklyn Bridge, 2000, 21″ x 34″, oil on canvas, Courtesy of Uptown Gallery.

Women and Fiction, 1991, 34″ x 55″, oil on canvas, Collection of Nicholas and Nancy Sander.

Quiet City, 1990, 48″ x 48″, oil on canvas, Collection of Sara and Richard Rosenstock.

Lovers, 1993, 40″ x 65″, oil on canvas, Collection of Myrna and George Weisenfeld.

La Lune en hiver, 1992, 34″ x 55″, oil on canvas, Private Collection.

Cat with Nudes, 1996, 30″ x 30″, oil on canvas, Collection of Carol Weston and Robert Ackerman.

Mother and Child Reading, 1993, 34″ x 34″, oil on canvas, Collection of Penny and Paul Schindler.

Rylona's View, 2000, 34″ x 34″, oil on canvas, Courtesy of Uptown Gallery.

The Common Reader, 1988, 34″ x 34″, oil on canvas, Collection of Bruce and Arlene Nadel.

Femme Lisant, 1989, 34″ x 34″, oil on canvas, Private Collection.

→ Credits ←

Anna Akhmatova: "The Poet", from *Selected Poems*. Copyright © 1976 by Ardis Publishers. Reprinted by permission of the publisher.

Margaret Atwood: "Psalm to Snake", from Selected *Poems II: Selected and New 1976–1986*. Copyright © 1987 by Margaret Atwood. Reprinted by permission of Houghton Mifflin Company and Oxford University Press.

Roy Blount, Jr., "Summertime and the Reading is Heavy", from *Now, Where Were We?*. Copyright © 1978, 1984, 1985, 1986, 1987, 1988, 1989 by Roy Blount, Jr. Reprinted by permission of International Creative Management, Inc.

Jorge Luis Borges: "Ars Poetica", from *Selected Poems*. Translated by W. S. Merwin. Copyright © 1999 by Maria Kodama. Translation copyright © 1999 by W. S. Merwin. Used by permission of Viking Penguin, a division of Penguin Putnam Inc.

T. Coraghessan Boyle: Excerpt from "This Monkey, My Back". Copyright © 1999 by T. C. Boyle. Reprinted by permission of Georges Borchardt, Inc., for the author.

George Bradley, "6 x 10 x ∞", from *The Fire Fetched Down*. Copyright © 1996 by George Bradley. Used by permission of Alfred A. Knopf, a division of Random House, Inc.

Italo Calvino: Excerpt from *If On a Winter's Night A Traveler*. Copyright © 1979 by Giulio Einaudi Editore, S. p. A., Torino. English translation by William Weaver copyright © 1981 by Harcourt, Inc. Reprinted by permission of the publisher.

Raymond Carver: "Reading in a Restaurant", from *The Collected Poems*. Copyright © 1996 by Tess Gallagher. Reprinted by permission of International Creative Management, Inc.

Anne Caston: "The Book", from *Flying Out With the Wounded*, Copyright © 1997 by New York University Press. Reprinted by permission of the publisher.

Miguel de Cervantes: Excerpt from *Don Quijote*. Translated by Rob Ackerman. Translation copyright © 2000 by Rob Ackerman.

Karen S. Chambers: "Reading Goals". Copyright © 2000 by Karen Chambers. Reprinted by permission of the author.

Jerome Charyn: "Word Music". Copyright © 1992 by Jerome Charyn. First appeared in *The Review of Contemporary Fiction*, Summer 1992. Reprinted by permission of the author.

Xi Chuan: "Books", from *New Generation: Poems from China Today*. Copyright © 1999 by Wang Ping. Translated by Wang Ping and Murat Nemet-Nejat from the Chinese of Xi Chaun, by permission of Hanging Loose Press.

Billy Collins: "Purity" and "Reading Myself to Sleep", from *Questions About Angels*, University of Pittsburgh Press. Copyright © 1991 by Billy Collins. Reprinted by permission of the author.

Robertson Davies: "Books are for Reading", from *A Voice From the Attic*. Copyright © 1960, 1972, 1990 by Robertson Davies, copyright renewed 1988 by Robertson Davies. Reprinted by permission of Pendragon Ink.

Rita Dove: "Maple Valley Branch Library, 1967", from *On The Bus With Rosa Parks*. Copyright © 1999 by Rita Dove. Used by permission of W. W. Norton & Company, Inc.

Umberto Eco: "How to Organize a Public Library", from *How to Travel With a Salmon & Other Essays*. Copyright © Gruppo Editoriale Fabbri, Bompiani, Sonzogno, Etas S. p. A. English translation by William Weaver copyright © 1994 by Harcourt, Inc. Reprinted by permission of Harcourt, Inc.

Anne Fadiman: Excerpt from "Never Do That to a Book", from *Ex-Libris: Essays of a Common Reader*. Copyright © 1998 by Anne Fadiman. Reprinted by permission of Farrar, Straus and Giroux, L L C.

Mary Gordon: "My Curtains: Snowbound", from *Having a Baby Finishing a Book*. Copyright © 1985 by Mary Gordon. Reprinted by permission of the author.

Rachel Hadas: "Teaching Emily Dickinson", from *Pass It On*. Copyright © 1989 by Princeton University Press. Reprinted by permission of the publisher.

Donald Hall: "This Poem", from *Old and New Poems*. Copyright © 1990 by Donald Hall. Reprinted by permission of Ticknor & Fields/Houghton Mifflin Co. All rights reserved.

Mary Stewart Hammond: "Listening to the Radio". Copyright © 2000 by Mary Stewart Hammond. Reprinted by permission of the author.

Elizabeth Hardwick: "On Reading", from an interview in *Paris Review*. Reprinted by permission of *Paris Review*.

Jane Hirshfield: "The Poet", from *The Lives of the Heart*. Copyright © 1997 by Jane Hirshfield. Reprinted by permission of HarperCollins Publishers, Inc.

Langston Hughes: "English B", from *The Collected Poems of Langston Hughes*. Copyright © 1951 by Langston Hughes. Copyright renewed 1979 by George Houston Bass. Reprinted by permission of Harold Ober Associates, Inc.

BASCOVE received her B. A. degree from the Philadelphia Museum College of Art in 1968. After graduation, she worked with publishing houses worldwide, providing cover art for such literary figures as Italo Calvino, Robertson Davies, Jerome Charyn and T. Coraghessan Boyle. For the past two decades her paintings have been regularly exhibited in Paris and New York, including the Museum of the City of New York, the Hudson River Museum, New York University, the Musée de Cherbourg, and the Grand Palais. Her work can be found in the collections of the Museum of the City of New York, Time Warner, the Oresman Collection and the Musée de Cherbourg. The first book of her paintings, *Stone and Steel: Paintings and Writings Celebrating the Bridges of New York City* was published by Godine in 1998.

has been set in Monotype Fournier, a digital version of a type cut for machine composition under the direction of Stanley Morison as one of Monotype's revivals of classic types in the 1920s. The Monotype face was one of two modeled on types cut in the eighteenth century by Pierre-Simon Fournier (called Fournier *le jeune* to differentiate him from his brother Jean-Pierre). The elder Fournier purchased the historic Le Bé foundry in 1730, but it was Pierre-Simon, something of a polymath among typefounders, who would go on to make the more significant contribution to the typographic arts, designing not only roman and italic text faces, but script types, ornamental and inital letters, types for musical notation, and a wealth of ornaments and vignettes. Fournier's work was expansively displayed in his justly famous *Manuel Typographique* (1764), which combined his types and ornaments in one of the more ambitious displays of typographic finesse of its day. ⟜ The current type bearing Fournier's name is notable for its narrow set width, crisp cutting, and perpendicular shading. The italic is characterized by a regular inclination, a significant advance upon the "conflicting angularity" of earlier Granjon and Garamond models, and clear evidence of an increasingly mathematical bent in the typographic thought of the period. Lean and sparkling, this elegant face is as admirably suited to illustrated books as it was when it was first designed.

→>─→>─◅─◅─

Design and composition by
Carl W. Scarbrough